A Classroom

of

one

Growing the Mentor Teacher/Student Teacher Relationship

By: Doug Robertson

First edition

ISBN: 978-1975739171

More info:
http://hestheweirdteacher.blogspot.com/

Book design: Y42K Publishing Services

https://www.y42k.com/publishing-services/

Cover Design by Dorothy Dean
https://www.dorothydean.com/

For Bethany, Matt, Veronica, and Jill,
You made me a better teacher. Now get out there and pay it forward.

For all student and mentor teachers past, present, and future,
Thank you for committing to strengthening and growing our profession.

For my wife,
Thank you for all the support in all the things I do.
I'd never be able to do this without you.

For the Weirdlings,
Thank you for finally falling asleep so Daddy could work on his book.
I love you.

Table of Contents

Foreword

My first day visiting the elementary school was a simple introduction day. I walked down the hall with the principal of the school. I was the last person in my program to be placed in a classroom and I was very nervous. For some reason it had taken a while for my program to find teachers for everyone in my cohort, which was disheartening at first, but all of my sadness evaporated when I got the email explaining that they had found a mentor teacher for me! The elementary school year was starting in a day or two, and I had no inkling of who this person was or what kind of teacher they would be. I remember walking through the door of the classroom and nearly stopping in my tracks. He had blue hair, his classroom was a mess and there was some kind of metal music playing. I didn't note what it was at the time, but looking back it's safe to say that it was Metallica. The principal left quickly and there we were, student teacher and mentor. He handed me a journal with Guiding Advice in 20 Parts and a really nice note. The first sentence: "Welcome to *our* class!" We talked for a couple of hours about his teaching experience and life and easily fell into a conversation about all of the things that we had in common. It turns out that we're both pretty big nerds. We quickly established that Star Trek, Star Wars, Mel Brooks films, super heroes, and you know, other nerdy stuff, were all super important and awesome. He then explained that he wanted me to leave this year with enough experience to feel as prepared as possible for my first year of teaching. I believe his exact words were, "So you won't drown." We talked about his expectations of me as a student teacher, and at that point my expectations of a mentor teacher had been blown out of the water, and I left with a huge smile and, for the first time since I started my journey to becoming a teacher, a feeling that I was truly heading for the right profession.

I remember the first day of student teaching with students in the room too. Doug, my mentor teacher and the author of this book, went over the classroom rules with the students. It wasn't a traditional conversation; you know the one, "Respect Others, Be Responsible, Be Safe." Those were important, and came up later, but they weren't the main focus of the conversation at first. He had the students come up with every rule they could think of, everything that would be important to remember when learning in a tiny room full of other humans. Some of these rules were pretty impressive. "Don't shove a pencil up your nose" and "Don't run around with scissors" came up naturally. After having the students come up with every rule they could think of, 57 in total, he worked with them to slowly bring these rules down to those three main rules mentioned earlier: Respect, Responsibility and Safety. He took it one step further and changed those three rules into one simple statement, because who really wants to memorize three different rules? That one rule was to "Be Cool". If it wasn't a cool thing to do or say, don't do or say that thing, and that stuck through the entire year. The students were impressed and thrilled at the entire process. He then said to the class, "This is OUR classroom, OUR shared stuff." Just those words gave every student (and student teacher) in the room a sense of ownership and belonging. These were nearly the same words he had said to me the day before, the first day I had known him. That was a magical feeling, to walk into a classroom and be assured that it wasn't just a place I was visiting. I wasn't just a guest. I was a part of that room, a part of OUR classroom. A part of MY classroom.

I spoke in front of a class of 36 students on the first day of school, which doesn't sound like a big deal, but to a first time teacher it meant the world. I introduced myself and had conversations. I walked around and played the Get-to-Know-You games and I loved every second of it. The classroom was full of energy and semi-organized chaos the entire year, and I watched as this group of amazing, crazy, and creative students grew into people who thought outside the box. People who solved problems in different ways and used materials, mostly cardboard and packing tape, to create amazing things.

I rushed to my classes the next week excited to tell everyone in my cohort about my teaching experiences so far, and to show off my new journal. I quickly discovered that I was standing alone with these experiences. Nearly no one else in my cohort had taught a lesson in their classroom yet. None came in with a really cool journal containing helpful hints. None of their teachers had blue hair, was a loud and proud Metallica fan (as far as they knew), or taught using monster puppets. I realized that I had won the jackpot of mentor teachers, and I was almost nervous to share my experiences because I knew mine wouldn't be like theirs.

I spent the year creating new lessons, solving student problems, using new tech that I had never seen before, learning the best way to cut cardboard, supporting students that needed extra time or extra attention, and, most importantly I think, I failed sometimes. Doug told me to break the classroom, meaning fail big, because it was always fixable. He essentially gave me permission to take risks. This was an amazing gift, and again, I knew I was becoming a teacher in a way that wouldn't be possible anywhere else. I did fail sometimes, but often I was successful. I learned to handle the kind of drama only 5th graders can create, and I learned to change a lesson that was teacher-led into student-led, project based presentations and performances. I was taught to look at a lesson and ask myself, "How can I make this better? Should I use tech? Find a way to use paper and tape? Movement?" Doug gave me feedback after nearly every lesson I taught, all the way through. His feedback was simple, one half of the page was full of "Likes", the other full of "Suggestions." This feedback, along with the little bits of advice I was given daily, helped to shape the teacher that I am today, and helped me to see the kind of teacher I want to be.

Mentoring a student teacher can't be an easy job, especially when you have an entire classroom of kids that need to learn a lot as well, but Doug took it all on without a second thought. I am so grateful for the experience and advice, and I know he has a lot to teach the world. He taught me how to teach the Weird Way, but he also taught me to become my own teacher. Without the experiences I had while teaching, I have no doubt that my upcoming year as a first year teacher would be a lot harder than it's going to be. I know that I am still going to have those first year teacher struggles, but I've learned that failing and growing from that failure, is a part of being a teacher. It's a part of learning, which is what teaching is all about right? Sometimes those failures lead to better lessons, or open the door to conversations that never would have happened before. It isn't easy to fail, but it's harder to have never failed, in my opinion.

This book is sure to be full of helpful hints and great advice for anyone that teaches, especially those who are thinking about or want to teach teachers. Mentorship was a huge part of my training, and without the key pieces of advice and experiences I had while student teaching, I wouldn't know what I was walking in to. Teaching isn't easy, but it is pretty magical, and being a student teacher gave me the unique experience of being on both sides of the desk, the side where I was learning, and the side where I was teaching. Both were essential, and I hope to never lose sight of the importance of being on both sides.

For those of you considering becoming a mentor teacher, I would encourage you to go for it. Being a student teacher is all about learning, but I know that I managed to teach Doug a few things as well. My mentor teacher helped get me started, and I am so grateful for the experience. I am sure that we are both better teachers for it, and I know that through these experiences I have started paving the way to becoming the kind of teacher I admired as a student. Mentor teachers are the next step in education, and student teachers are more than eager to learn from you and grow. So go for it! I know I'll be taking on a student teacher some day when I have experience and techniques of my own, and I can't wait to see what they will teach me.

-Veronica Miller
Oregon, 2017

1. Pebbles in the Pond

It is impossible for a teacher to find the edges of their influence. Like a pebble thrown into a pond, the effects of a teacher on a student's life create ripples far beyond the point of impact. Concentric circles of ideas, lessons, and feelings growing and changing as they interact with other ripples.

A teacher rejoices in those ripples. Education is a long game, and often the things we do have far-reaching consequences. We never know which of the things that happen in our classrooms will be remembered, half-remembered, or simply folded into the subconscious. Think back on the way you feel about things, the way you think and learn. Can you pinpoint all the influences, all the ripples in your life that brought you to this moment?

I have chosen to have student teachers in my classrooms as often as possible because I want to make the biggest possible ripple. As immodest as this might be, I believe the things I do in my classroom, the ways I teach, have value. If I didn't, I wouldn't be teaching that way. I also believe in education. I don't need to be called an influencer, awakener, thought leader, or other fancy term- I am a teacher, and I am proud of it. And as a teacher, I see it as my job not only to educate students, but to strengthen my profession as a whole. Education isn't a contest. It's not a competition and, as I'll get deeper into through this book, there's not One True Way to teach. It is not about me being better. It's not about my class being the best. It's about all of us growing. I see it as my job, our job, to help the teachers of tomorrow into the world of education.

I am a pebble in the pond of my students' lives. By taking a student teacher, I am widening my ripples, as well as throwing another pebble into the water. I've never expected a student teacher to teach my way. But I do expect them to internalize the philosophies of joy, creativity, excitement, and leaping after ideas with wild abandon into their own practice. I want to help student teachers learn to make their own ripples.

This book is written for veteran teachers who are thinking about taking student teachers, and for students considering the call of the classroom. It's for mentor teachers taking their first student teacher or even their fifth. It's for students who know their place is in a classroom. I want to share what I've learned having student teachers of my own, and having watched and listened to the experiences of other student teachers and mentor teachers. In this way I hope to help grow the profession. I hope to strengthen it.

For those just joining the profession: Welcome. This is unlike anything you've ever done. You are about to say and do things you never thought you'd ever say. You will form sentences no human in the history of Earth has ever spoken aloud. "If you don't stop snapping your fingers, I'm going to take them away." You will ride the roller coaster of emotions that is teaching a lesson. "They're not getting it. Wait, that was a good question. By Jove, I think they've got it!" You're going to clean Target, Walmart, and your local grocery story out of markers, glue, folders, and pencils. In February. Because that's when the supplies from the beginning of the year run out. Do you enjoy having normal conversation with your friends and family? Warn them now, because they are about to hear all about this kid in your class that did a funny thing- you see he said it like this and that's funny because last week this other kid did this thing after recess and she also- hey where are you going, come back.

I mean all of that in the best way, because this is the greatest job. You student teachers are about to be paid to hang out with kids all day. Kids are the best people on Earth. Kids are much better than grown-ups. And not because of that, "Children are just so honest" hooey you hear people who don't have experience with children say, but because they're hilarious and ever-changing. Teaching is never the same from day-to-day. Every lesson is different, every day, every year. You will, hopefully, never teach the same thing the same way twice. You get to do something, reflect on it, change it, improve it, and then do it again. Or, as Monty Python puts it, "it's time for something completely different," but using all that stuff you learned before. Teaching is a living thing because we work with students. Buckle up, it's one wild, wonderful ride.

For those taking on student teachers: Thank you! Thank you, thank you, thank you. Thank you for choosing to take a baby teacher under your wing and guide them into this wonderful profession. Student teachers reading this are going, "Hey, 'baby teacher'?" Yes. Mentor teachers are educational midwives, easing your transition from the collegiate womb to the outside world. Thank you for taking the risk, time, and energy to split yourself yet one more way. Thank you for putting ego aside. For though we don't admit it, ego can play a big part in how we teach and why we choose to do certain things. If this is your first student teacher, prepare for the most transformative experience of your teaching career. It was for me. I have learned more during the years I've had student teachers than at any other point in my teaching life. Taking a student teacher means taking another look at everything you do, everything you say. Doing it well, being the best mentor teacher you can be, means first modeling true reflection. Being willing to hold all your practices and philosophies up to the light, turn them this way and that, and see the strengths and flaws.

Thank you for strengthening the profession. Colleges and universities with student teacher programs, in my experience, struggle mightily to place their students. I was given a student teacher the day before the year started once because the university could find no one. Imagine being that student, in a program, wanting to learn, but twisting in the wind. By agreeing to have a student teacher, you have said, "Yes, I do have something to give back." That isn't always the easiest thing to say. Kids are one thing. College students, future teachers, that's different.

Thank you for showing compassion and giving that which is most precious to you, your students, over to someone brand new so that they may learn.

Some might imagine this book should be split into sections: Student Teacher and Mentor Teacher. They would think that I'd organize it like these are separate acts. I don't believe they are. Education is a holistic experience. Some chapters will be more heavily weighted toward the student teacher experience, and some more heavily weighted toward the mentor teacher experience, but the nature of the relationship is such that one cannot exist without the other. We are in this together, and this book is written that way. As mentor teachers, we must keep the needs of the student teacher in mind. And student teachers must do the same for their mentor teachers. Much like teaching, our classrooms are more of a handshake than a pointed finger, so is the partnership you're now a part of.

To get terminology squared away here and now, I know programs like to say cooperating teachers and guest teachers or teacher candidates rather than mentor teacher and student teacher. In these pages we're talking about the field experience, so I'm going to call the relationship what it is- student teacher and mentor teacher. Those are the terms we're using and, students, if your university says different you can secretly know they're wrong. Cooperating teacher sounds like an apology, "Thank you for cooperating with us." Cooperation suggests that the relationship is between the university and the classroom teacher. It's not. The university is the middleman. The relationship is between the classroom teacher and the student teacher and, done right, that is a mentoring relationship.

There will be a lot of story-telling in this book. It's also, as you've already noticed, written from my perspective, like I'm talking to you. This is how I learn, and it's how I teach. If you're looking for a formal text, you've chosen the wrong book. Hopefully, you're looking for a conversation, an attempt at understanding and connection that goes beyond what many sterile education books want to do.

Together we are the pebbles in the pond. Together we can make waves.

2. Why Should I Take a Student Teacher?

Taking a student teacher is the most valuable thing I've ever done as a teacher. I learned more the years I had a student teacher in my classroom than any other year. I became a stronger teacher those years than just about any other. It challenged my beliefs, helped my students, and allowed me to impact the profession in a larger manner. That's why you should take a student teacher.

Wouldn't it be wild if I actually ended the chapter there?

The reasons most teachers are resistant to taking on a student teacher are, for the most part, good reasons. They make sense, especially to the person making them, as most excuses do. Let's pick through the most common excuses not to have a student teacher and look at them from all sides. Student teachers reading this book- this isn't a chapter for you to skip. If you've been nodding along so far that means you're buying in, which means I'll have homework for you later. You'll need this list again.

I don't have the time/It's a busy year

Yep, it is. At the risk of alienating my audience right off the bat, I know we don't really have the time and it's a busy part of the year. But we *never* have enough time and it's *always* a busy part of the year. When is the year not busy? Think about the school year- too busy because it's the beginning of the year and we're still catching up, because stakeholder conferences (aka Parent-Teacher Conferences) are coming up and so are report cards, because this is that rush between Fall break and Winter break when there's so much to cram in, because Christmas break is coming, because we're trying to catch back up from Christmas break, because The Big Test At The End is coming and we need to be ready, because The Big Test At The End is here, because there's report cards to do and we've gotta catch all those standards we didn't get to already, because it's the end of the year, because it's summer and break and no one has student teachers over summer break, what are you crazy? I know. I work in an American public elementary school. The year is always crammed full and bursting at the seams. At some point that has to stop being an excuse.

Now, I want to be clear here- I am not advocating teachers taking on more work for no pay, but this is different than sitting on another committee or chairing another initiative. Universities compensate mentor teachers in different ways, often with professional development credits which, if you're like me, lighten another load. I'd rather worry about a student teacher than about filling out more paperwork and going to one more online class.

This isn't busy work. It's not just one more thing. It is, not to get hyperbolic on you, taking the future of education into your own hands. Aside from teaching the students in your classroom, there's nothing more important professionally. You don't have to do it every year, In fact, I don't recommend that. Take time between student teachers to rest that part of your skill set and apply the lessons you learned. Life Truths: You're never actually ready to have a child. You never actually have enough time in the school year. But both things still get done.

I don't have anything to offer a student teacher

I get so fired up by this one. Pretend it's not you. Pretend it's another teacher telling you this. Another professional educator looks you in the eye and says they don't have anything to offer a student. I can hear you starting to protest, "That's not what they're saying!" But it is. The operative word in student teacher is student. Saying you don't have anything to offer a student teacher means you think you don't have anything for a student. You're wrong, by the way. Do not sell yourself short. I'm not going to pretend even for a second that you don't have anything to offer a student. You obviously have taste and a desire to learn. You're reading a book about teaching.

Modesty is a hallmark of educators everywhere and it's not always a good thing. We consistently sell ourselves short. One of the reasons we get pushed around politically is because we're unwilling to step away from clichés and openly say, "I'm good at this job, and I deserve to be treated like a professional who is good at their job. I am an expert. Recognize." I've been in so many meetings where we try to go around the room and get ideas from each other on what to do and teachers will bashfully shake their heads, "I'm not doing anything special." Liars! Lying liars telling lies! You are! I know it. I know that if I walked into your classroom, I'd see you doing something I've never thought of. I'd see you teaching in a way I never have. I'd find things to steal (no, not borrow, I'm not giving it back, I'm stealing it. If stealing ideas makes you uncomfortable, then I will trade you for it. I have a cookie in my lunchbag). Admit it, you are doing good work, and we can learn from you. If you believe students can learn from you, then you must believe teachers can learn from you.

I think a lot of this is Imposter Syndrome coming out. Every single one of us, the tall and the small, is pretty certain someone is going to find out that we're faking it. Sure, we know the book stuff and we look like we know what we're doing, but a lot of education is still getting by on instinct, which is really the combination of experience, training, and luck. If we let a student teacher into our rooms, then we'll be exposed as the frauds we really are!

Might be projecting a little there…

Anyway, student teachers need a place to go. A place to learn. Your classroom can be that place. This isn't about impressing someone who has taught for two dozen years or getting observed for an evaluation. It's about preparing someone to step into their own classroom a semester or a year from when you get them. You have those skills. You have something to add, something to share, something to put back into the system. Have faith in yourself.

I'm actually an alien posing as a teacher in order to learn more about the human race

First: Welcome! I hope you're enjoying Earth. Depending on where you landed and when, you'll notice we're in a kinda weird place right now. Sorry about that. We're working on it. Please don't tell your superiors we're all as messed up as the select few you might see on the news.

Second: What better way to maintain your cover, learn more about human interactions, and begin spreading pro-alien propaganda than by taking on a human apprentice? This is a win-win. You're welcome.

I had a bad experience with a student teacher before

Getting a placement is a crapshoot for both the mentor teacher and the student teacher. Personalities may clash. Styles may differ. It's a gamble. But it's still worth putting in your chips.

I have been lucky enough to have been given hard-working, dedicated students, driven to become great teachers. There were a few times with one that we had to have a Serious Conversation, but those times were few and we quickly solved our differences and got along great afterwards. I realize this is not the experience of everyone. I have a friend who recently had an experience with a student teacher that could best be described as the Hindenburg, but worse and with more explosions. She would have every right to be gunshy about taking another student teacher. The cooperating university did what they could, but the kid did not have what it takes and also did not have the emotional maturity to either find what it takes or be honest with himself about his lack.

This will be a reoccurring theme, so highlight it now: **The operative word in student teacher is student.** If you wouldn't make the excuse about a student in your class, you shouldn't make the excuse about a slightly larger (or much larger if you teach the tiny human grades) student in your class. Sometimes kids come to us unwilling to learn. It's our jobs to find ways to reach them. If the student happens to be in college, the only difference is that we can't call mom and schedule a meeting. We can call the university supervisor, but that doesn't have the same kick. But we've all had rough classes. Classes where you love the kids but, man oh man, when they're all in a group there are some interesting chemical reactions happening. Classes that at the end of the year we sit back and think, "That was something else, and I loved them but I'm glad it's over." Those classes didn't drive you from the classroom. So let it be with student teachers. Join me in the optimistic view that people are good, and believe the odds are ever in your favor. Many programs will even let you meet the student teacher before you accept them. This is one more level of self-protection. Don't let one bad experience rob students of the chance to learn from you.

I'm in a testing grade

My friends, we cannot continue to use standardized tests as reasons not to be the most creative, flexible, excellent teachers we can be. Before you fire up your email machines, I know many districts still weight the tests more heavily than is fair. I know we report scores up the food chain and administrators hold our feet to the fire. I know test scores are one of the myriad ways non-educators try to wrest control from us. I do. I've never not taught a testing grade. Every year since the beginning of my career, I've dealt with the joy that is days of sitting quietly, trying not to peer over shoulders and, "cough readitagainslower cough cough." Every year I tell myself my quality as a teacher is divorced from the scores of my students on a test I didn't even design while simultaneously praying to Examinus, the god of assessment, that they do well and *make me look good.* The struggle is real.

The risk that student teachers will twist that all up is also real. In one of nature's cruel tricks, The Big Test At The End comes right around the time when most student teachers are supposed to be fully taking the reins. This is because Examinus has a sense of humor and is also kind of a jerk. If I'm going to be judged based on my test scores, then why should I entrust part of the instruction of my students to an unknown quantity?

Put simply- because they aren't alone in the room, and because by the time the Big Test At The End comes along, the student teacher should no longer be an unknown quantity. **If the operative word in student teacher is student, then the operative word in mentor teacher is mentor.** So mentor, guide, help, and assist. Having a student teacher does not mean you hand them the keys, wave goodbye, and go get coffee (but you will occasionally stop and grab coffee for two on the way to school because you're a cool person like that). Even deep into their year, our student teachers still need our help. Co-planning is still happening. Guided reflection is still happening. Interventions are still in place. You are still in it together. Mentor teachers are in the room so a student teacher can mess something up completely and the mess will be cleaned up just as quickly as it was made. Mentor well and your test scores will not suffer.

I'm in a testing grade. I have to use All the Data too. This is a learning experience for the student teacher. When your student teacher gets hired, they might get hired into a testing grade. The student teaching year is all about gaining that kind of experience with a net beneath them, so when the net is gone they already know how to balance the demands of teaching.

My admin something something something

All of this is contingent on having a good administrator. I've realized that when it comes to being happy at a school the one factor more important to me than any other is a high quality administrator. An administration based on trusting the teacher is vital. An administrator should know that things in a classroom with a student teacher might be a little messier than a classroom without one, and that's ok because there's even more learning going on. Learning is a messy business. A strong administrator will allow student teachers to get all the emails, sit in on all the meetings, get to know the real nitty-gritty of the job. All the things that aren't Teaching but still take up space on the plate.

Taking on a student teacher automatically means taking on more responsibility. Hopefully you have an administrator that understands that and is supportive of your choice. This is a person that is regularly on the lookout for new hires. They should be thrilled that a teacher on their staff is doing their part to make an administrator's job a little easier by training a new teacher up well. A good administrator will know that as a mentor teacher, your plate is pretty full. And a good mentor teacher will stress the importance of balance to their student teacher. It is here that I'll admit that I'm a total hypocrite about all this. I'm all about saying yes to taking on more work because I want cool things to get done at my school. One year I had a student teacher, took the lead on the MakerFaire, and sat on School Site Council, along with all the normal joyful madness that happens in my classroom.

We did a ton of great work that year, and my student teacher learned a lot. We both also slept for two weeks once summer break started.

At the end of the day, anyone can come up with a list of reasons why they shouldn't take a student teacher. This chapter could go on forever, as humans are endlessly creative when it comes to getting out of work. But the gains outweigh any cost. The growth and reflection. The reward of strengthening the profession. The benefits to your students by having another adult in the room to learn from, another adult whom they can teach. It's not easy, but by taking a student teacher, you can directly impact the growth of another teacher, and in that way impact every student that teacher has through their career.

Also, by the end of the year, you'll be able to leave the room to pee whenever you need to instead of waiting until recess or lunch. This might be the best reason.

3. Journals and Big Rocks

Congratulations! You have been given a student teacher or have been placed with a mentor teacher! Your shared journey is about to begin.

Now what?

Now you're building relationships. Now you're getting to know each other. I want to set our relationship off on the right foot, so I give my student teachers a gift- a journal. A journal is the perfect gift for a student teacher because it welcomes them to your class, but also communicates that we're here to work. Buying it for your student teacher says, "I expect you to take notes and reflect on what happens this year, but I will be here to support you." It is a tangible thing that, used correctly, can be of use to your student teacher long after they've left your care.

The journal comes wrapped in our first Talk. We talk about the purpose of the journal, and this leads us to the topic of self-reflection. I explain that we will have many conversations about things that happen in the classroom, and I forget things all the time, so I write them down. If they don't need to write things down to remember, that's great. But this is the tool to use if they do. They will want to go back, reread, rewrite. They'll want to be able to grab the journal and jot down an idea. They'll use it after every single lesson they teach and during every lesson they observe. I had a student teacher who used the back pages to keep track of all the ridiculous things I said throughout the year because apparently I'm full of them. Yes, it's low tech, but that's good. The tactile writing of things- having it on pages- that's a goodness. This is coming from someone who takes notes almost exclusively with his phone. Except when I'm writing student teacher observations. I want paper. I want to write in the margins. There's something special about a journal.

I write on the first page of the journal. We're sharing this journey, this knowledge, and so we are sharing the beginning of the journal. We're, quite literally, in it together. Or I'm like my oldest child and am capable of giving a gift only if I get to use it first. One of the two. I don't write some inspirational quote or happy note. This is meant to be used for work, so with my first act I try to cover all the basics I'll want to get deeper into as the year goes on. Below is the list of nineteen things I put in my student teacher's journal before handing it over. In italics next to each item I have explained my reasoning. The reasoning doesn't get written, it comes through during many conversations over the course of the year.

1. **DON'T PANIC!**

No book, fictional or otherwise, has a better beginning than The Hitchhiker's Guide to the Galaxy. *Right at the start of* The Guide *in giant letters you'll find those two words- Don't Panic. So you can say that putting DON'T PANIC first is good advice, and also a little test for me to find out if the person knows the reference. A way to find out if there's an immediate, easy connection we can make. Pop culture is the grease that eases friendships along. It's also good advice in general, since as a student teacher, there will be plenty of chances to panic, and panicking is the last thing you'll want to do in front of a classroom.*

2. **Remember: They are children**.

It's easy to forget what this means. We get to work with kids and help them grow, but they are kids. They will make kid mistakes. They will say and do things that, to an adult, seem bonkers. Odds are good that a student teacher might not have spent much time around little ones prior to being in a classroom, so the reminder helps. Don't dismiss things as too simple. Don't forget Mary Poppins finding the element of fun to help her charges along.

3. **Discipline the behavior, not the child.**

Discipline is the number one thing student teachers worry about. "What if they won't listen to me?" This piece of advice is a guiding light to live by, and one I still remind myself about regularly. The child is not broken, the child does not need fixing, don't make it personal. The choice is the problem, the behavior is what needs to be examined and replaced. Keeping that front and center will act as a compass in stormy seas.

4. **Your classroom will reflect you, for good or bad.**

When you go into a room and it feels light and bright, that's the teacher. When a room feels oppressive, that's the teacher. I am constantly asking my students why I always end up with the weirdest group of kids. They are constantly giving me significant looks in return.

5. **When in doubt: The Beatles.**

Music is always good in class, and The Beatles are the best. Aside from some drug references, many of which are so well-written as to go unnoticed by all but the most astute student, the songs are clean and no parent or administrator will complain. If you need a break, throw on The Beatles. I'll add another band to this- OK Go. They make the best music videos in the business and if you're looking for a way to kickstart creative thinking, OK Go videos are the bee's knees.

6. **Steal. Others have already taught this.**

We're getting better at this as the internet opens the world of education to us. There are plenty of crafty-type websites with all kinds of resources. The trick then is to instill in your student teacher the understanding that no lesson is ever ready-made and easy to use out of the box, no matter what the box says. Download it, but then get out your whiteout and red pen, because there is editing to be done. Still, it's easier than creating something whole cloth, especially if you're starting out and don't even know where to get the cloth. Couldn't hurt to ask if there's a P.O. for that or…

7. **Learn from them, laugh with them.**

I wonder how many student teachers come through college without realizing how fun this job is. Are methods classes so wrapped up in the How To aspects of teaching that they never stop to talk about the joy of education? I know most new teachers are so petrified of messing up that the laughter gets lost. It's an explicit goal in my class, with my student teachers, that they understand the fun. Embracing the fun will get you through a lot that could burn you out. It's a cliché to say that a teacher is also a learner, but most clichés exist for a reason. Every student in the room has things to teach us, so be willing and be open to that. Nowhere in education does it say the teaching can't go both ways. Model being a learner. This goes for student teachers with their students, but also mentor teachers with their student teachers.

8. **Fear may motivate, but love inspires.**

I tell this story every chance I get, and it's because we can learn as much from a negative example as we can from a positive one. In Hawaii I worked with two of the meanest teachers you've ever seen. They called themselves, and I'm not making this up, Hammer One and Hammer Two. They shared students for reading and math. If you got in trouble in Hammer One's class, you knew that when you got to Hammer Two's class she'd know about it and you'd hear it all again. Once, one of my students described the definition the word "suspense" by saying, "It's like going to [that teacher's] *class. We know someone is going to get in trouble, but we don't know who or why." But you know what? Their classrooms were quiet. Work got done. Students sat straight in their chairs. They performed well on tests. And they hated school and were scared to go to class. If a student loves you, they'll try. They'll go above and beyond because they aren't scared of what will happen if they stumble. They'll play. If a classroom is a place a student associates with play, then it's a place they'll want to be. So you can be The Trunchbull and it'll work, but wouldn't you rather be Ms. Honey and let the learning sing?*

9. **They will rise to your expectations, but they may also need a boost.**

High expectations of students are important, because they will work to what you expect. You will learn that you have no idea how capable most students are, so don't underestimate your students. Let them show you how smart and able they can be. But kids are coming from different backgrounds, starting in different places, all needing different things. We're talking about equity, not equality here. To level the playing field so everyone succeeds some kids will need more help than others. That's not favoritism, that's being a good teacher and a compassionate human.

10. **Why blame the parent? You aren't teaching the parent.**

It's so easy to blame the parent. And it's almost always bull. Blaming the parent means that you, the teacher, think you're better than they are, you think they don't love their kid enough or correctly, that they aren't doing their very best. Too often blaming the parent is a crutch, an excuse for why we can't reach the kid. Don't do it. It's also a gateway to allowing yourself to be blind to honest reflection.

11. **Say please and thank you. You are the example now.**

Manners manners manners. I want my students to be polite, because I want them to be productive and functioning members of society. I want them to have opinions and change the world too, but please and thank you grease those wheels. Plus, you already have all the power as the grown up. Don't be a jerk. Please. To go along with this, I wouldn't expect students to call you "sir" or "ma'am". I realize this is a cultural and regional distinction, but I feel it creates a divide and yet another power differential that might get in the way.

12. **Allow yourself to be amazed someone trusts you with all these tiny people.**

It's crazy that we get paid to hang out with kids, build stuff out of cardboard, read stories, and program robots. That's our job. We get to do that every single day. That's freaking cool. Embrace that.

13. **Volunteer to coach, help, and lead.**

School does not start when kids arrive and stop when the kids leave. Schools run on teachers working hard and helping out early and late. We should get paid more, we should not be going outside contract hours, we should get paid extra for extra work. But we should be doing the extra work. This is a dual reality of teaching. Mentor teachers- your student teachers see when you don't do anything to help the school as a whole. They will learn that schools aren't communities, they're islands if you do this. Please don't. Plan things, grow the community, help out. Model how to be a member of a strong, supportive staff. If enough student teachers see this and internalize it, soon every staff will be like that.

14. **Speak up in meetings, and have faith in your own opinions. Rock the boat. Promote change.**

Education isn't perfect. It's nowhere close. It's rife with systemic inequality, bias, and supremacy. It's constantly evolving, as it should, because education is all about knowledge, and knowledge should be everchanging. Student teachers- you have ideas, you know things, you are the next wave. Don't be stifled because you're "just a student teacher" or are "too young to know better." You may tell yourself that, and others may say it to you. Push through that and do what you know is right. Take your instincts and try them. Mentor teachers- we should encourage this risk taking. It's the risk takers that move the profession along. Be a part of that. There are ways to tactfully and diplomatically challenge ideas, and part of a mentor teacher's job is to help find those paths.

15. **Try not to complain about your kids too much. Negativity is sneaky and contagious.**

Dude. So easy to do, dude. So easy. It starts as jokes. You don't really mean it, right? Except, would you say it to the kid? To the kid's parents? If it was your kid would you want someone else saying it? Is it still funny then? Think of these jokes like we think of racial jokes- if you have to glance around before you say it, you probably shouldn't say it. Plus, you say something enough times and it becomes true. Yeah, you're kidding about that kid being dopey, but why do you keep saying it then? Not only that, but it spreads like a virus, infecting everyone. Negativity can poison your mentor teacher/student teacher relationship, and it can poison a classroom. Venting isn't really a thing. If there are problems, face those and look for solutions. Too many teachers' lounges are sites of competitive and contagious complaining. Rather than cede the space, be the vaccine with positive statements and good humor.

16. **Ok, sometimes you can blame the parents.**

This is mostly on the list as a joke. The dichotomy creates a humorous situation, you see. But every once in a while you'll have a student who comes from a situation where it's clear there are things going on at home that need to be dealt with. We're mandated reporters. If you don't know who to talk to, go to your counselor, if your school has one, or your administration. No one wants to get this call wrong, but no one wants to miss the call either. You report, then let people who have the training take it from there. Better to be wrong than to be right and silent. That stuff echoes loudly in classrooms. Blame still isn't the correct word, but the idea is sound.

17. **Be prepared, be comfortable, be flexible.**

Know what you're going to teach. Student teachers- do not think you can wing it. You cannot. You won't even be Icarus, who flew too close to the sun and crashed to Earth for his hubris. You'll be Icarus's buddy no one ever talks about, who didn't take the time to build his wings right, leapt from the building, and immediately became a smear on the pavement below. Don't do it. Preparation makes you comfortable. You've seen presenters who were wound tight and locked into their presentation. Don't do that. Teaching on the rails does not allow for authentic learning. Know your stuff, but relax into it. This is easier said than done. Flexibility is key. Build escape points into lessons. Know how to get out in case you see a teachable moment or your kids aren't getting it. And be ready to tap dance because you have no idea what students are about to throw at you. Mentor teachers- you might be comfortable being flexible, let your student teacher gain this skill too. That's not something they should learn when they're alone in their own classroom.

18. **Be able to justify everything you do.**

Especially once you start getting creative. When kids are crawling around on the floor, cutting out cardboard and using miles and miles of duct tape, the child better be able to explain to your principal what they're doing and what they're learning from it. Which means you have to be able too. But it's more than that. When I say be able to explain everything, I mean everything. From the desk arrangement to the seating chart, or lack thereof, to why the projector is where it is and why you stand where you stand when you teach. Mentor teachers- this is on us. We model this. A massive part of our job is justification. Student teachers should be asking why, and we better have answers. Student teachers- cultivate this skill now because it will come in handy come job interview time.

19. **Don't worry, the teacher next door is faking it too.** - *Seriously. We've all got Imposter Syndrome. Remember that social media and presentations (and books) show the best face of the person who created them. Anyone who claims to have teaching nailed down is lying, because students change every single day. It's a constant exploration and adventure. Embrace that.*

Big Rocks

The items on that list are what I call the Big Rocks of teaching. The term "Big Rocks" comes from a story I heard when I was a lifeguard-in-training, and it's the perfect metaphor for teaching anything complicated. The story goes like this-

A professor stood in front of his class and pulled a jar out from under his desk. "Is this jar full?" he asked. The class said that no, it clearly wasn't full. So the professor pulled a box of big rocks out from under his desk and one by one stacked them in the jar until no more would fit. "Is it full now?" he asked. Some students said yes, now the jar is full. The professor again reached under his desk and this time brought out a box of smaller rocks and pebbles. Without speaking, he poured the pebbles and rocks into the jar, where they filled the nooks and crannies the larger rocks left open. "Is it full now?" he asked. The class was wise to him and said no, it was not yet full. Pleased, he reached under his desk and pulled out a box of sand (some tellings have him pulling out a jar of water.). He poured the sand into the jar, where it found all the still smaller holes and finally filled the jar.

This is learning. Our knowledge is the jar. We start by learning the Big Rocks, filling up the major gaps. That's methods classes and the first few months of student teaching. You wouldn't teach someone who'd never ice skated before how to do a triple axel. First you'd teach them to properly lace their skates. Big Rocks. Eager students, and this goes for student teachers and the students you're in front of, love love love going straight for the Small Rocks. Kids think hypotheticals are the best. Which is great, except it pulls them away from all the learning they need to do to properly understand those hypotheticals. It takes forever to fill up a jar using only Small Rocks. Good, motivated student teachers love to ask questions that can be answered, but that they aren't quite ready for. Which is great. That's what the journal is for. Write those questions down, we'll come back to them. I will often tell my student teachers we're working on Big Rocks right now. When I observe lessons I'm looking for Big Rock issues. When we're planning lessons we're looking for the Big Rock ideas first. It is a common refrain in my classroom, "Big Rock!" It's shorthand for my student teacher and me. It says, "That's a good question, and we will get there, but not quite yet."

This book is made up of Big Rocks and small ones. I believe we should be explicit and honest with our students, and tell them what kind of rocks we're working on. We should also let the students know that further exploration on their own, the personal excavation and discovery of Small Rocks, is one of the most joyous parts of the learning process.

4. Starting out on the Correct Foot

The part of the school year before the kids get there is a whirlwind of activity- box checking, copy making, meeting attending, and panic attack having. I'm hoping that at some point it gets easier, but I've been through over a decade of them now and it hasn't yet. Part of that is probably how often I've moved around, because each school and each administrator has their own system. You can be as, "I'm an independent punk rock teacher who fights the power and disrupts the system, maaaaan!" as you want, but at some point the secretary will chase you down and force you to do that paperwork. A school is a machine, and that machine runs on paper and procedures. But each school defines paper and procedures a slightly different way, and it's your job to find a way to work inside that. This starts with the pre-student days of school. There are signs to be made, websites to update, lessons to plan, and spreadsheets of schedules to stare uncomprehendingly at until someone on your team holds your hand and patiently tells you how to read it for the third time. That last one might just be me.

Schools are systems within systems, wheels within wheels, and every teacher has a system to set up and prepare the year. Some teachers set their classrooms up the same every year, as a baseline. They've been in the grade long enough to know this goes here, that goes there, and this will all run smoothly. Some teachers are more like I am, where every year is a new adventure and a chance to try something new. My classroom will be similar to the previous year's, but it won't be identical. I will have had some idea at some point during the summer and suddenly I spend an entire prep day on the floor with a drill, taking the legs off all my desks. (This is not hyperbole. Floor desks are cool. Anything that throws kids and parents off just a little on the first day is, in my opinion, a good thing. Sends a message right away that this school year will be different).

My system always starts, and I swear this is true, with me flat on my back in the center of my room, staring up at my ceiling, trying to envision my room and push positive energy into it. I realize that sounds very go-hug-a-tree-here's-your-crystal, but classrooms have an energy all their own and your energy impacts it. Don't knock it. In Hawaii the staff was convinced some of our classrooms were haunted. Hawaiian folklore includes ghosts, so they brought in a Hawaiian priest to bless the rooms. I don't even believe in ghosts, but it still changed how the rooms felt. Classrooms have energy. The system builds that energy.

Then the student teacher arrives. Hopefully their program gets them into a classroom at this point in the school year, or before. Now there's this other person in here with me, sharing my space. Touching my stuff! Of course, it's no longer mine. It's ours now. **Remember: The ultimate goal of a mentor teacher is to prepare the student teacher to walk into his or her own classroom as ready as possible.** To accomplish this, the student teacher should be a part of all aspects of teaching. Including the stuff away from student contact, when we are preparing for student contact. That's a lot of the stuff that isn't taught in college courses.

So now you're in your classroom with your student teacher, trying to prepare the room. A student teacher can be like a puppy- cute, great to have around, but always underfoot. Student teachers- we like it when you have the energy and enthusiasm of a puppy, but when there's a System, puppies often disrupt that. This isn't a complaint. We asked for this. The disruption is part of the fun of having a student teacher because disruptions force reflection. One of your most powerful tools is your ability to question. You should be taking in the teacher's system from setting the classroom up and asking why these desks are like this and what are those folders. Make your mentor teacher justify the choices being made, because we mentor teachers have sometimes forgotten why we're making those choices. Some things become old hat, it's what we do because it's what we do. That isn't to say that we're unwilling to change, but sometimes it's hard to notice when things have become set in stone. A choice becomes a habit and like a stream over rock, over time a groove is formed, a groove that grows deeper and harder to get out of.

Mentor teachers- we must encourage them to question everything. They do not know, and it's our job to guide and help. Do not brush questions aside. Do that too often and your student teacher will learn their questions will get no answer and have no value, and that will ripple through their teaching long after they're gone from your room. I'm not suggesting we need to change everything for our student teachers. I am saying that we should answer their every questions to the best of our abilities.

There is a thing that happens on TV shows like police procedurals, science fiction adventures, and doctor dramas where while a character is doing their job they are also explaining what they're doing out loud in detail to other characters. "What I'm doing now is reversing the polarity of the tachyon flow into the neutrino reactors, which will cause a quantum flux and solve the problem we've been having in the generator coils." These exchanges should always end with the explaining character saying, "But you know all of that because you work here." The explaining, of course, was for the audience's benefit. As the mentor teacher plans, we should be that character from the show, over-explaining every step until the student teacher is able to say, "But I should know that because I work here."

This classroom setup time is also the feeling out portion of the student teacher/mentor teacher relationship. This is when we're setting norms and habits that will continue for the rest of the year. I ask my student teachers if they have opinions on how the classroom should be set up. That first time, most don't. They probably haven't seen an elementary school classroom since they were in fifth or sixth grade. But the offer is there. That piece of our relationship is now established- I want your opinion. I want you to speak up. Your voice has value. And if the student teacher does have an idea I'll try it. Or I'll say, "That's a good idea, but not for this point in the year. Hold on to it, write it down in your journal, and we'll come back to it." Small Rocks and Big Rocks.

To the super-organized teachers out there who have taken a student teacher- you are intimidating. Not on purpose. But you've got your thing and it's locked in and looks unassailable. This is where I beg you to step away from the pre-built lesson plans. That's not an effective learning environment for a student teacher to grow in. We're balancing the learning of our students, which takes precedence, with the learning of the student teacher. We must find a way to get those two things to work in harmony. What doesn't do that is handing them the stack of copies you always make for the first month of school and saying, "Here's the first month of school." I know you think you've got this down to a science, and this might be where we come to a philosophical impasse. But that kind of preparation is only helping you, the teacher. It isn't what's best for the kids, and it isn't what's best for your student teacher. How can you know what the first month will be like until you meet your kids, get a feel for how the class meshes together, and find the most natural pace? Should that tender time be entrusted to a pre-planned packet?

Perhaps this is my own little soapbox and I'm standing by myself. Perhaps that method works better in the lower grades, where I've seen it done, than it does in upper elementary and beyond. But I'll forever contend that a classroom should not be on rails. The watchword in any classroom is flexibility. One phrase I say over and over until it's mantra for student teachers is, **"Never be hardline about anything except not being hardline about anything."** Making the year easier for us, the teachers, is not the point. It never is the point. Student teachers- it's great when things are easier for you as a teacher. Don't count on it happening unless you force it. This isn't an easy job. If you want a job where you can predict the future and dictate what's going to happen, be a director or a computer programmer. Teaching is not that job. Mentor teachers- don't lead a student teacher to think that this can be perfectly planned out. Don't simplify teaching. It's anything but simple.

I'm not saying don't be organized. Be organized. I'm not, but that's all me. I subbed for the most organized teacher in California regularly and it was always the easiest and most stressful job of the week. She had color-coded folders for each day and subject, all hanging nicely in a box. Subbing for her was a matter of, "Go to the red folder. Inside the red folder there is a purple folder. This is math." Way easy day. But still not on the rails. She was a good teacher and was constantly flexible. She knew what was going to happen, but was able to change how her class would get there.

So again, mentor teachers, I beg of you, don't make this seem easier than it is. Student teachers have to see all the behind the scenes work in the room where that work happens. They need to see how the sausage gets made. Leaving aside for a moment the idea that some teachers make reams and reams of worksheets to start the year *shiver*, we still have to justify to our student teachers why those copies exist and how they are beneficial. Student teachers- please push your mentor teachers to justify those things. Worksheets aren't always awful, there's a time and place for just about every learning tool, but it's not a tool you want to use too much.

All of this is taking place before the kids even get to the room. Together, the mentor teacher and student teacher build a rapport that's the starting point and baseline for everything to come. You both discover a working relationship and rhythm. Hopefully you're lucky and you mesh well together. You find common interests. Nothing makes teaching and learning easier than forming a relationship at the outset. You're about to do that with your class, you should do it with each other. Everyone deserves the kind of start my last student teacher and I had. We were exchanging email addresses and when she told me hers a lightbulb went off in my head. "Wait, is your email a reference to Seven-of-Nine from Star Trek: Voyager?" I asked her. "Yes!" she replied. "We are going to be best friends," I shouted at her, pulling out my phone to show her the picture of my dad and me with William Shatner from the Star Trek Las Vegas conference I'd been at a few weeks prior. (Note- no one gets that lucky. Forget seven of nine, that was one in a million). Find common ground. Mentor teachers and student teachers don't have to be the best of friends, braiding each other's hair and having sleep-overs, but you will be working together for the better part of 180 days. I suggest finding ways to take it beyond a purely professional relationship.

Part of planning those first few days is figuring out how to involve the student teacher in the proceedings. The first week of school is a delicate thing. There's a lot of teaching that needs to be done before any teaching can get done. The first week of school is all training students in the rules and procedures of their new classroom. In my room, it's a cooperative effort. I want the students to have ownership of the class. The moment they walk in the door it ceases being *my* class and becomes *our* class. And like I said, when there's a student teacher in the mix, it is never *my* class, it should already by *our* class. We're in this together. Everything I do with the student teacher at the outset is geared toward making it clear that, while with me the operative word in student teacher is student, **with the kids the operative word in student teacher is teacher**. I do not introduce my student teachers in a way that makes them seem less than. I do say, "We're very lucky this year because we have a student teacher. Does anyone know what a student teacher is? Yes, a student teacher is a teacher who is learning to be a teacher. We have one of them. Instead of one teacher, you get two this year." Then I ask my student teacher to get up and introduce him/herself.

This is key, and it's also something I can't believe I have to stress, but I know it doesn't happen: **Your student teacher should be talking to the class from Day One.** Please do not make him or her this shadowy figure in the back of the room. What's mine is yours and my class is your class and I expect you to feel ownership of it. I expect the kids to see you as a teacher and treat you as such. So we start the year as co-teachers. My student teachers teach a lesson on the second day. I know this is unusual because I've spoken to other students in my student teacher's cohorts. They've shared horror stories with me about their classmates not saying anything to the class for weeks at a time. About the mentor teacher tossing off an introduction and then moving on. This is the exact wrong way to start the year.

Mentor teachers- take the time before the year starts and discuss with your student teacher how she/he will introduce him/herself. Help talk her/him through the proper tone to set. Many student teachers will be too stiff or wooden, and others, like I was, will be too loose and friendly. The line that we walk between being their friend and being their teacher isn't clear and isn't easy to see. It takes work. Workshop the introduction. Script it out if you have to. The time it takes will be worth it when you see your class accept the student teacher as a natural part of the class. Your student teacher deserves the respect of your class. But, like everything else, you must model that. I am proud to have a student teacher. I am proud that my students will be the ones to shepherd my student teacher through this final phase of their journey. I say that in those words out loud to our students, their parents and guardians, and anyone else who asks.

Student teachers- advocate for yourselves. Ask ask ask ask to be in front of the kids. Make sure your mentor teacher knows you want to introduce yourself. Come in with a Getting to Know You lesson idea for the first week. Everyone hates ice-breakers at meetings, but they can be fun games in the classroom. Get out of the way of your nerves, which will be telling you, "This isn't a good activity. My mentor teacher probably has a better one. I don't need to bring this up." You know what? Your mentor teacher probably does have a better one. That's why they're the mentor teacher and you're the student teacher. That doesn't mean yours doesn't have value. I'd rather have a student teacher with spunk and energy, bringing me ideas, than one who passively waits to be told what to do. Teaching is not a passive activity. Learning is not a passive activity. You might be a shy, introverted person. You're still going into a profession where you must take stands, push ideas, be who you are. It'll be a challenge. An understanding mentor teacher will remember that you're a student, and you're not supposed to have all the answers yet.

Part of the introduction process means making sure the parents and guardians know you have a student teacher as well. You are now co-headliners. My letters to parents aren't signed, "Mr Robertson and friends." They have my name and my student teacher's name. Once I have my student teacher writing the letters their name gets to go first. Be proud that you are bringing another educator into the world, and show that by making it clear to any who ask that this is your teammate and partner.

If the operative word in student teacher around the mentor teacher is student, and the operative word in student teacher around students is teacher, what about mentor teacher? It's both, because obviously the mentor teacher is teaching the student teacher to teach. But more importantly **when the mentor teacher is with their student teacher they are a mentor**. You're the guide. The student teacher should be looking to the mentor teacher, but the mentor teacher should be proactive. Teacher mentorship is in short supply. Proper mentorship would prevent a lot of burnout. A mentor gives support, ideas, and a gently guiding hand. A mentor is available for talks. A mentor teacher does not stop being a mentor just because the student teacher has left their classroom.

My first long-term teaching position was as a four/five combo teacher in an overflow classroom. The fourth and fifth grade classes at this school were too full, but the number of students over the cap wasn't enough for a new fifth grade class and a new fourth grade class. It was enough to form a four/five combo. So I, a brand new teacher, was tossed into a class that was created mid-year out of students that were pulled from the classes they had been in. I'll be honest here- combo classes, in my humble opinion, are *no bueno.* They're exponentially harder on everyone. I was woefully unprepared to handle this. It went very badly. I was so terrible that even writing about it makes me feel ill. I want to find all those students and personally apologize to them. I wasn't abusive or anything, I was just embarrassingly bad at teaching. And I knew it, which made it all the worse. I would get back to my apartment at the end of every day and cry, not figuratively or metaphorically, but for real with real tears and gnashing of teeth, about how bad I was at my job. I had help from one or two other teachers at the school. But my real help was one of my former mentor teachers. I called her and we would go to dinner and she'd help me plan and figure out discipline plans and lessons. I knew I could call her because we'd worked so well together when I was in her second grade class. She was great, and she made a bad situation more bearable. This story, by the way, doesn't have a Teacher Movie happy ending. I sucked until I was done in that position. But the next time I taught I sucked less. I've also never taught a split again. I'd rather take baths with a man-eating shark, or wrestle a lion alone in the dark, eat spinach and liver, pet ten porcupines, than tackle the split class my admin assigns.

A mentor never stops being a mentor. Time and distance don't matter. Take the title seriously, mentor teachers. We have the chance to change the world. The ripples of a mentor teacher are more meaningful than we'll know.

5. On Observations

Watching someone else teach gets old and boring fast. Trying to learn to teach by observation is akin to trying to learn to swim by watching a swim team workout. You'll notice Big Rocks, and eventually you'll be attuned enough to pick out Small Rocks, but for the most part you'll be bored out of your mind, and your muscles will not cooperate with your brain when you try to put your observations into action. Watching someone teach isn't motivational. No one gets excited to go to work and watch. None of us got into teaching to watch. We got into teaching to do.

It is at this point that I will subtly note the obvious parallels here between how we treat our student teachers and how we run our own classrooms. *long, significant look*

The tendency of mentor teachers is to go with a lot of Watch This first. This gives us the chance to get the class settled into routines and used to our style. It also, we tell ourselves, gives the student teacher a chance to get acclimated and, much like the students, learn the rules and routines. We think, "Modeling is good teaching, so model I shall. And the student teacher shall like it." Forgetting that the other thing we're modeling is a Sit Down And Shut Up learning style.

To a student teacher, this is engaging for all of a day, maybe a day and a half. Much like a classroom is often artificially well behaved those first few days of school- that period of time where the students are getting over their nerves at a new grade, a new teacher, new experience of having a long-haired, blue-haired, tattooed, loud man teacher who uses puppets (that last one might be a little too hyper-specific) - so too is a student teacher artificially well behaved at the jump. That's not to say that most student teachers or students aren't well behaved, but nerves and newness normally result in a stiff unreality. Personalities don't shine through until the teacher demonstrates that personalities are ok. I mentioned before that I always have the weirdest group of kids in the school. Part of the fun is watching those kids come out of their shells as they notice I encourage their individual voices.

A new student teacher knows they are in a precarious position. They need their mentor teacher more than the mentor teacher needs them, and everyone is acutely away of this natural power imbalance. Without the mentor teacher, the student teacher can't pass their college classes, can't move forward to the next phase. In most cases this pushes the student teacher into their best behavior. Not in all cases. As mentioned before, I had a friend whose student teacher was the opposite of helpful and willing to learn. I don't know why someone would waste an opportunity to learn like that, but sometimes a senior in college isn't as mature as you and I might think. These are the exceptions, not the rule. Thusly, a student teacher will do whatever is asked of them, especially if what is asked of them is, "Sit there. Watch me." That's easy. It might even be a relief. Student teachers- you'll be new to the classroom, new to being around kids like that, and you may feel like an entire colony of caterpillars are emerging from their cocoons in your belly. Nerves are to be expected. What a load off, then, to be told to sit off to the side and watch.

For a day it's a load off. Maybe two, if you're really dedicated to the cause. But there are only so many notes to take before eyelids get droopy and the mind wanders. (Again, this might not just be a lesson for student teachers. *longer significant look*) It's hard to focus sitting back there all by yourself, watching someone else do the work. At this point everything is a Big Rock because you don't know what you're supposed to be watching for. You desperately try to take everything in, and in doing so miss everything important.

Mentor teachers- we must give student teachers focus. We cannot assume they know what they should be doing much like we don't assume our new students know how the room works and what is expected of them. The rule is to never assume a student knows, but to fully explain and remove all doubt. It's worth the early time investment and saves headaches and confusion later. Tell your student teacher specifically what they should be looking out for. "For the next hour I want you to watch how I move around the room." "For this period watch how I call on students and respond to them." Narrow-focus goals will keep your student teacher's mind sharp. It will guide their note-taking. Think about how you would correct a student's essay. You could mark it up, correcting every single mistake and painting the paper red, but that's discouraging and overwhelming. Instead you tell the student that first we're going to focus on spelling or grammar or supporting details. Yes, you'll need to get to all that other stuff, but it's easier to correct things a bit at a time.

Student teachers- for note taking I recommend a three column chart, like below:

Notice	Questions	Other

Note the headings of each column. They should be fairly self-explanatory, but as you read a moment ago, it is better to be absolutely clear.

The **Notice** column is for you to write down anything you notice about the specific Big Rock your mentor teacher asked you to focus on. No matter how small, no matter if you think it is related but aren't sure, write it down. It's better to ask. You never know what you're picking up that's more important than you realize. Also, you never know what you're picking up that your mentor teacher doesn't realize he's doing. That is when you get to see real learning and reflection happen, when you point out something we've been doing so long we don't notice it anymore and we're forced to explain it. Mentor teachers- we will explain it too, or explain why we can't and why that isn't ideal.

Questions is, well, for questions. The Whys and Whats that pop into your head as the lesson goes along. Try to keep these focused on the Big Rock of the moment. Do not assume that you'll remember everything you see and think. You won't. There are a million things happening in a classroom at any one time. Teaching is exhausting work, and your brain will be toast by the end of the day. Write it down. Let the journal remember for you.

Other is for anything that comes up that isn't part of your direct observation but pricks your brain enough that it should be written down. It's good to have an Other section during note-taking like this. Your brain is like an RPG game character, collecting every piece of information along the path because you never know what will be a key. Save these things, bring them up in the later conversation, see what you can craft with the new information. You might save yourself some time later on.

Mentor teachers- our job is much the same, but trickier. Observing someone when the power dynamic is tilted in favor of the observer is intimidating for the person being observed. We've all been there. The principal comes in and parks it in a convenient chair (yet another reason I like having alternative seating in my room- it confuses adults and I like confused adults), opens her laptop, and starts typing away. You're up there in front of the kids, or hopefully down amongst the kids as they control their own learning, and you're just supposed to continue on as if nothing is happening. Because I like subverting expectations, when my principal walks in I'll often call out, "Principal is here! Everyone pretend to be learning!" or I'll have the class turn and wave to her. An administrator's job is hard, I'm just trying to lighten things up. Of course, in my head I'm saying, "[Insert Child's Name Here], be good be good be good."

In those situations I think of a famous 1984 story about the greatest baseball team ever, the Los Angeles Dodgers. Third baseman Pedro Guerrero had committed several unusual fielding errors during a game. This was during the same time that Dodgers' second baseman Steve Sax was undergoing a well-publicized fielding slump in which he couldn't throw the most routine ball to first without something going wrong. In the post-game meeting, Dodgers manager Tommy Lasorda went to Guerrero. "What are you thinking out there," Lasorda asked. "Two things," Guerrero said. "What's the first thing?" "God, don't let them hit the ball to me." "And what's the other thing," Lasorda asked. "Don't let them hit the ball to Sax either."

Anyone who's had the principal start to make the slow rounds of the classroom knows exactly that feeling. Keep that in mind as you observe your student teacher.

Whenever your student teacher is in front of the room you should be taking notes. We should also be giving the student teacher things to think about and focus on. Veteran teachers sometimes forget the massive amount of information we're processing at any one time. We've got a dozen subroutines running in the back of our heads constantly, noticing sounds, movement, the confused looks, suppressed giggles, the air of the room. Student teachers don't have that. Especially at the start, then they only have The Lesson Plan and they cling to it like Jack would have clung to the door if Rose actually loved him. As when I suggest that student teachers should be given a specific thing to focus on when they watch us, we must have a specific thing to watch for when we watch them. The student teacher should be aware of what that thing is. Then the conversation at the end of the day isn't full of surprises.

Later on, as the student teacher gets stronger, I have the student teacher tell me what I'm to observe. Student teachers- it is important that you are able to communicate a goal to your mentor teacher. When I was a young person I was on a swim team. My mom got me a one-on-one private lesson with the head coach, Coach Lisa. Coach Lisa was, to put it simply, an intimidating woman. Great coach, but scary to my young self. I showed up to the private lesson and Coach Lisa asked me what I wanted to work on. "I dunno," I said. This did not go over well. She went on a long, I wouldn't say diatribe, but it also wasn't a calm explanation of facts, about how this was *my* time to learn anything I wanted and why would I waste that time having no goals. "You know what you need to work on better than anyone," she said. "Why didn't you think about those things before you came here?" And she was right. This lesson has never left me. I must take responsibility for my own learning. Student teachers, you must take responsibility for your own learning. So as soon as you are able, you will tell your mentor teacher what you want them to look for. Your mentor teacher might have other things to watch for as well, but the onus is still on you.

Mentor teachers- We must be present in the learning of all of our students, the tall and the small. To guarantee I am for my student teacher, I use this:

Likes	Suggestions

The **Likes** column is for things I see that the student teacher is doing well. Could be within the goal or outside of it. It could say, "Using the timer," or, "Handled that distraction well." I write in short statements that are quick to record but still clear enough for my student teacher to use when I'm not around to interpret.

Suggestions are things I see that could be improved. They aren't weaknesses because the student teacher is learning. I'm suggesting improvements. "Lesson took too long." "Tied to the board." "We should have figured out how to get the kids moving here." Suggestions reflect that the lesson being taught was planned together, and there are often things I see that I should have noted during that phase. It's not judgement, it's modeled reflection. This also makes clear that the student teacher doesn't have to take my advice. I am not The One True Fount Of Teaching Truth. But I am in the room, and I do know things. I don't write in full sentences because I'll be explaining myself more fully later. Speaking of not having to take my advice, these two charts are not the only ways to take notes, obviously. They work the best for me. You find what works the best for you.

I will often find myself drawing arrows between columns. For example, if in the Suggestions column I write, "Move around more." And then the student teacher does, I will draw an arrow to Likes and note, "Good, started moving." This gives me a chance to give real, useful feedback that reflects the realities of what is happening in the classroom moment to moment. I can tell my student teacher that it's good they did move, but it could have happened sooner. Some administrators call this a Correction Sandwich- start with a positive, then the correction, then a positive. This works especially well with students and parents. What I described above is more of an Open-Faced Correction Sandwich, but flexibility matters. I'll also note a Suggestion like, "Should be more student movement in this." Then I'll follow it up with an asterisk, "*I should have noticed this during planning." We're in this together. That's why there's no Mistakes column.

The chart is specifically labeled Likes and Suggestions because Likes and Criticisms or Likes and Dislikes are entirely too negative and aren't constructive. Suggestions is a more exacting reason for the chart and the observation in general. It's also less intimidating for a student teacher when I tell them I'll be taking notes. As we remember from being observed by our own administrator, observations are never as stress-free as you want them to be. Not at first. Student teachers- get used to being observed. It will happen your whole career. Learn to welcome observations as a way to strut your stuff and your students' learning. But that's a Small Rock skill. For now these aren't so much observations as they are constant and consistent learning opportunities. They will happen every day, because yes mentor teachers, **thou shalt let thy student teacher teach at least one thing every day**. And it will be Instructive for them and the students. Handing out a worksheet, running reading assessments, doing attendance, these are not Instructive. Have them do those things too, but not as the main work.

Student teachers- you will also make yourself some form of a Likes and Suggestions chart for the lessons you teach, and you will honestly reflect when your lesson is done. It will be instructive for you and your mentor teacher to see where your lists converge and diverge. Your mentor teacher will give you the few minutes it takes to jot these notes down when there's a gap.

Moment of honesty- I get distracted easily. My mind will wander. I started using the Likes and Suggestions two-column chart as a way of keeping myself honest and on top of it. I know myself well enough to know that one- I will forget 90% of what I wanted to talk about if I don't write it down and two- I might start to doodle or get distracted by an email or watch a kid instead of the student teacher (yes, we're watching both at all times, but this is about the student teacher right now) if I don't have something to do.

However, note-taking is not enough. It's never enough. You have to talk about these things. Every day.

Every.

Single.

Day.

At the end of every single day my student teacher and I sit down and discuss the day. We go over our notes. I let my student teacher choose who goes first, and we have a guided conversation about the day's work. How else are you going to get better? By guessing? No. You are in my class to learn, I am calling myself your mentor, so I had better act like it.

I'll be honest, this seems like a no-brainer to me. Taking notes and then debriefing at the end of every day feels like the most natural part of being a mentor teacher. It's how I teach. Feedback, direct and immediate. It's how I learn. But I've heard stories about mentor teachers who don't give specific feedback to their student teachers. Who don't watch or take notes. Who *leave the room to make copies* WHAAAAT No no no no no nein no no nope no no nope. No. A student teacher is not an aide. They aren't a teaching assistant or a paraprofessional or push-in support. A student teacher is a student under the care of a mentor teacher. A student teacher is a classroom of one within a classroom of dozens. And a student teacher deserves to be treated as such.

These conversations are where your student teacher will

learn to be a reflective professional. These conversations are where you together start to fill their jar with Big Rocks and collect the Small Rocks. These conversations are there to supplement to the notes your student teacher has been taking the whole time. The conversations make your notes mean something. Every once in awhile we'll skip the conversation. There's a meeting after school, one of my children has a doctor's appointment, my student teacher needs to get to class. Be flexible. But that's not the habit. It should get to the point where neither of you feel the day is complete without having had your short debrief. These conversations are where you assess progress towards goals and prepare new ones. The fact of the matter is, just like your students should never be surprised by the grades on their report cards, your student teacher should never be surprised by their evaluations. They've been evaluated openly and honestly the entire time.

Constructive criticism can be hard to give. Especially when a lesson goes well. I always find something. A great lesson is a perfect time to pour in some Small Rocks. There is no feedback more useless than, "That was great. Good job." There's nothing actionable there. Don't pick nits, but you know there's something to focus on.

All of this takes time. Good things take time to do well. Learning to teach is hard. Teaching someone to teach is hard. Being a mentor is hard. The days will be longer than those of many of your colleagues, except for that second grade teacher that's in her classroom until seven pm every night doing science-knows-what. Since this is apparently the chapter where I tell sports stories, we'll finish with one more baseball quote, this one by fictional ball player and manager Jimmy Dugan. "It's supposed to be hard. If it wasn't hard everyone would do it. The hard is what makes it great."

6. Widening the Scope of Not Sucking

Student teachers, come closer. I need to tell you something. A truth that isn't always easy to hear. A truth that carries the embarrassment of reality within itself. Ready? Listen closely-

Everyone sucks at teaching when they start out.

Everyone feels like they suck at teaching at multiple points during their career...the school year...the week...each day sometimes.

This can crush a person's soul and will to go on if not dealt with in healthy ways. New teachers are especially vulnerable. The attrition rate for new teachers in America is alarming. It's not the "half of new teachers quit within five years" statistic you hear thrown around sometimes. That's just something people say to sound frightening. You can't believe those kinds of statistics. After all, "63% of all statistics are made up on the spot, and most quotes are either misattributed or completely made up." Gandhi said that. You wouldn't argue with Gandhi, would you? I thought not.

Teaching is a job filled with enormous pressures. Pressures placed on us by our administrations, by the state, and by the federal government. Then there's the the more important pressures placed on us by our parents, our students, and ourselves. These always come first. Sure, yeah, Big Test At The End, blah blah blah, but I'm more concerned about my kids. This attitude about The Big Test At The End drives some teachers batty. Eye on the ball, your kids are more important than some test will ever be, no matter what. Don't be stressed because you think you should be. You will be more concerned about your kids than the test too, because you will understand that teaching exists without an administration, a state government, or a federal department. To be clear, I'm pro-all those things. I'm public school and proud through and through, but my point stands. All teaching requires is a student. They're the only thing that really matters, and you will worry yourself sick over each and every one of them.

This means that it's much too easy for teachers to be much too hard on ourselves. A good student teacher wants to be a great teacher. You know the opportunity you are being given is special, and you understand what it must feel like for your mentor teacher to hand the reigns over to you and let you learn with their kids. Take note, because words matter: We rarely say, "my students." We say, "my kids." Those are my kids you're teaching, so you better be on it.

Is your stomach tied up in knots yet? Ok, now take a deep breath and give yourself a shake, because I am going to talk about the mechanics of sucking at something.

There are levels to sucktitude. Sucking at something is never black and white. You're *supposed* to suck at something you're new to. Again, this is an idea that directly relates to the students you will be teaching. You would never expect a student who has never seen a fraction before to be able to add it, subtract it, simplify it, or turn it into a decimal. So why should you, who has never taught someone to add, subtract, simplify, or convert a fraction before be any good at it? I'll tell you why you think you should. You feel the enormous weight of the educational edifice pressing down upon you. Your thoughts cascade against each other, toppling like dominoes. *Oh man, if he doesn't learn to add fractions now then next year he'll be behind and he won't be able to catch up and that means every year after that he'll fall further and further behind and then he won't get into college and something terrible will happen and it'll all be because in third grade I sucked at teaching fractions!* OR maybe you're worried that you'll be marked badly on your review by either your mentor teacher or university supervisor and that bad lesson will mark the beginning of the end of your educational career. OR maybe you're not one to be quite so dramatic and you simply stress yourself out because you want to do a good job and you know you're not doing one and that ties you in knots.

Let me take you in my arms, like Robin Williams held Matt Damon in the Hollywood classic **GOODWILL HUNTING**, and tell you, "It's not your fault. It's not your fault, Will." If your name is not Will, then this is still true, just use artistic license and swap your name in. Matt won't know. It's not your fault you don't know exactly what you're doing. That is, in fact, why you're a student teacher. To practice teaching until you do know what you're doing on some basic, general level. At the very least. I plan for my student teachers to leave me much more than generally prepared. That, though, comes with a lot of time in front of the kids, struggling through. Learning. Exploring.

Working out is all about tearing down muscle fibers so that they rebuild themselves stronger. You have to break things (gently and safely) in order to rebuild them. Your mentor teacher is your lesson spotter. We make sure you aren't lifting too much, but we can also tell when you aren't lifting to your full potential. Like an athlete, it helps if you talk to us. Remember those daily meetings I mentioned in the previous chapter? That's when you bring up your fear of sucking. That's when we talk about it.

Mentor teachers- know that your student teacher isn't going

to be great at this right off the bat, and keep in mind that you knew that going in. Keep in mind you weren't great at it at first either. Think back. We can't get frustrated with a student teacher who is trying and making mistakes as long as the mistakes are always new. Now, if your student teacher makes a mistake, you correct it in the daily meeting, and they continue to make that same mistake, then frustration sets in. But your skills as a mentor teacher kick in as well. You will look at the student teacher as a student who isn't getting a concept and rather than think, "What's wrong with this student?" you'll think, "What's wrong with how I'm teaching this student?" Student teachers- that's a Big Rock lesson in teaching too. It's your job to find a way for the kid to learn. It's your job to help the kid see it's their job to learn.

Mentor teachers- also know all that "You're gonna suck," stuff I started this chapter with isn't actually all that motivating and your student teacher doesn't need to hear it on the regular. I hate it when veteran teachers fill new teachers' heads will all kinds of negative rubbish under the guise of doing them a favor and keeping it real. It's spreading poison and it's not helpful. It's harmful. There's a difference between honest talk and sowing fear:

- Honest talk: Yep, teaching is hard. Yep, you will get better, but it will take time, and some pieces will take longer than others.
- Sowing fear: Ugh, this job is so exhausting all the time and these kids today and their parents and the testing and boy oh boy this generation it's so hard to get their attention and woe is me.

This job is awesome and the good always outweighs the bad.

It's always worth it- even the sucky parts.

Let's widen our scope of what sucking is. That's why the narrow focus goals during lessons and observations are important. That's why we're learning Big Rocks first. Because we are successful in stages, and each stage is complex and more difficult than the last. We did not go from Kittyhawk to the moon in a matter of weeks or months. There were many phases to that journey. It also didn't take us that long in the grand scheme of things. The first time man flew in an airplane was December 17, 1903. That first flight lasted a mere twelve seconds and Orville only traveled 120 feet. Neil Armstrong set foot on the moon July 20, 1969 after traveling over 238,900 miles, a journey that took 75 hours and 56 minutes. One hundred and twenty feet feet to 238,900 miles in only sixty years. I don't even want to think about, or Google, how many failures, crashes, and explosions there were between those two flights. Man sucked at flying for a really long time. But part of the reason we kept sucking at flying is because we kept trying to fly further. We could have stopped at 120 feet and just gotten really good at that distance. But where's the joy of learning and discovery in that? Part of the reason you'll never be satisfied with your teaching is because you'll always be trying to teach better. You'll constantly be re-evaluating lessons and projects and the ways you present ideas. That's not actually sucking at something then, that's steady improvement. That's new mistakes, and new mistakes don't count as sucking.

I run a project early in the school year called The Hobby Project. The directions for the Hobby Project are simple- Each student must choose a hobby she or he would like to learn. It must be something they've never done before. Every night they must document what they did and how they felt about it. They have a compressed timeframe, about four weeks. I want my kids to go from zero to as far as they can get in a month. Projects and assignments are like a gas, they will expand to fill the given space. Compress the space. Students take up juggling, or ventriloquism, or knitting, or sewing. I had a kid start to learn to ride a unicycle, and another learn card tricks, and others dive into American Sign Language. This project makes the learning process tangible, immediate, and measurable. Assuming the child completes the documentation as assigned, he or she has a running record of going from sucking at something to sucking less at that thing. Now, in a month they won't be perfect. Perfect isn't the point. The point is to learn something brand new so they prove to themselves, without me having to hit them over the head with it, that learning a new thing is hard but possible. The point is that they are bad at something for a while and that's ok. But if they're motivated enough, and they are because they chose the thing, I didn't, they move themselves through the rough points. Often without realizing that's what they're doing. I widen the scope of what sucking at something is in my classroom and make it ok.

Fun coda/unintentional result to the Hobby Project story: The best project was by one of my Those Kids. A great kid, smart, funny, but I knew his name and had said it out loud a dozen times before recess on the first day. Struggled to make good choices. Lots of conversations with Mr. Robertson. He came in with the most incredible card trick I've ever seen. He had banter and he blew the class away. I sent him to other classes to perform it. I tried to send him to the office to perform it but he refused to go because going to the office had never been a good thing. He went from being That Kid to The Magician because of one project. This wasn't on purpose and I take no credit, except to say that it was the freedom of the project that let that happen.

Mentor teachers will be ok with the learning curve. Student teachers will find a way to be ok with the learning curve. We grow together. First time mentor teachers will probably suck at parts of mentor teaching. Sucking at parts is why I take notes. I sucked at focus and remembering. I solved the problem and grew. This is one of those times when a mentor teacher's job is as much to correct as it is to say, "It's cool, you'll get them next time." In my classroom I say, "Go ahead, break them a little. It's ok. That's why I'm here. I will help put them back together again."

Change the narrative around sucking at something. It's not a bad thing unless you never learn anything from it.

7. Seating Chart Fun

There are some things that need a gradual release of responsibility and some that can be handed over sooner rather than later. How quickly a student teacher takes on responsibilities are between the student teacher and their mentor teacher, but both should be pushing the other.

Student teachers- you should feel uncomfortable taking over certain areas of the classroom. That discomfort comes from the unknown. It's a good feeling, it makes you alert. It's motivating when it's not allowed to overwhelm.

Mentor teachers- that discomfort comes from handing over control of your room. Which means you still haven't accepted the truth that is it no longer *your* room; that the both of you, student teacher and mentor teacher, have had shared ownership of the space since the very first day. That's the only way for a student teacher to feel as safe as possible, and it's the only mindset that will allow a mentor teacher to give over as much control as is required for the student to learn.

On top of all this, of course, it's important to remember that ownership of the class doesn't actually rest with either of you. It rests completely with the kids. That's language that should be used with them on Day One. This is not *my* class, this is *our* class. Your students spend 180 days here, six to eight hours a day assuming you're in elementary school. The amounts change for middle and high school but the principle remains the same. It isn't a place they're visiting. It's not a hotel room. It's their room. It should be a space as important to them as their own bedroom.

It's where they go to learn and discover and fail and risk and try, so it better be theirs to own. It's also the place where the student teacher will go to learn and discover and fail and risk and try. So it's theirs too.

Mentor teachers- You have a set of rules that your class is run by. You have procedures. And now you're working with your student teacher to redefine and reimagine them. That's the first shared responsibility. Just giving a student teacher a set of ready-made class rules doesn't teach anything, just like telling your classroom, "There are the rules," doesn't give them a stake. This is a conversation to be had, first with the student teacher and then with the class as a whole. "What do you think the class rules should be?" Make a list. Check it twice. Figure out what makes a kid naughty or nice. Fine-tune it.

**whispers* Mentor teachers, hey. Meet me on the next paragraph. Student teachers *Jedi hand wave* you do not see the following paragraph.*

Just the mentor teachers now? Ok, good. You're probably still going to end up with the same rules you always have. At least to start. I let my students choose our class rules, but I also know what our class rules are. I've got them on laminated signs in my desk. But I'm going to let the kids come to them. We'll talk about all of the, "Don't do this," and, "Make sure you always do that," things that kids know a classroom needs. As we go I'll be nudging and combining, "Hey, this rule and this rule seem the same, can we put them together?" Do that with your student teacher too. Nudge. Rule building and early planning is like bowling without gutter balls, so we need to be bumpers. The trick is learning when to take the bumpers away and let your student teacher throw it into the gutter. Because they will. And that's ok. They get another throw. (I was going to say, "They get another ball," but recess duty has ruined me for that and I'll never stop giggling if I have to say, "Grab your balls and put them in this sack," one more time).

What other things can be handed over early aside from rule creation?

Yard Duty

If you've got yard duty, that's a thing they should be doing with you, so it's not really something that can be handed over. Student teachers- don't you be trying to get out of this grunt work. Yard duty, bus duty, cleaning the teacher's lounge fridge, these are all regular duties of a teacher so get used to it now. No mentor teacher wants to see you shirking. You could run the best math lesson in the world, but if you aren't willing to stand in the sun and make sure children don't get heated in an overly-competitive game of three-on-three, then you're in for a shock once you get your own room.

Morning Work

I have morning work in my class. Some teachers call it Daily Five. It's just about the only worksheet my students ever see, and it's the main reason I use the copy machine. Every day starts with a short half-sheet of language arts problems. This keeps the kids busy and shifts their brains into gear while I go about the morning routine of attendance and whatever else needs to be done. Student teachers- you'll be doing attendance soon too, if you aren't already. There's literally no reason for you to not take that over on the third day. It's easy.

Language arts morning work is grammar checks, sentence editing, that kind of thing. As a transition from recess to math, during snack time, we have a math sheet, still called morning work because "after recess during snack work" is too clunky.

This is the first quote unquote teaching thing I hand over to my student teachers. It's easy, impossible to break the class with, and low impact academically, which means if the student teacher teaches something wrong it's easy to fix without a whole bunch of backtracking. My morning workbooks also come with an answer chart, which is handier than you might imagine. Commas are tricksy buggers, and you student teachers haven't thought about proper semi-colon use or the why behind certain grammar rules in a decade or more. Same with math, only moreso. Chances are good that you learned the How of math, but not the Why. The Why is what we're going for now, and that leads to more questions than answers. Getting a little stuck on the morning work is good for a student teacher because it teaches you to say, "You know, I'm not sure. Let's look it up." Not knowing will happen all the time. Model being ok not knowing things and how to find out. My students hear me say, "Luckily, I have a MATH BOOK full of MATH and since this is a MATH question I have I should use the INDEX in my MATH book." All caps out loud isn't actually shouting, by the way, it's humorous emphasis. It takes practice. Mentor teachers- we sit in the back and monitor and take notes during this. We provide assistance as needed. We check the back of the workbook for answers and make noises like, "Huh, I didn't know that," so the students know the student teacher not knowing it isn't some kind of personal failing. We watch the kids to see who is spacing out and who isn't giving the student teacher the due courtesy. We sneak around on light teacher feet and provide proximity reminders.

Automatic Tasks

Like attendance, student teachers should be given any of the automatic tasks a teacher does on a day-to-day basis that cannot be done by a student. That's key, student teachers- don't do things the kids can do. You'll run yourself ragged. Pencil sharpening should be a job. Let a kid do it. But as student teacher you can assign the job. Mentor teachers- you're going to want to say, "But the student teacher doesn't know the kids as well as I do." First, these are things that can be handed over so early in the year that neither of you really know the kids all that well yet. And secondly, if the student teacher doesn't know the kids that well, giving students jobs is the perfect way to expand their familiarity.

Lines

Walking in line is another one of those school things that changes depending on the grade level, the school, and the type of teacher you are. Personally, my kids need to be in a straight, quiet line because they shouldn't be in the way of any other classes in the hall, and they shouldn't be disturbing other classes by talking as they pass. But that's it. Some teachers are militant about lines- close quarters, hands clasped behind the backs, bubbles in the mouth. Before I say the next thing I want to reiterate that I don't teach the tiny ones so maybe I don't know something, but I so very hate the bubbles in the mouth thing. I know, it's a way to help the littles remember they shouldn't be talking, but it's so demeaning sounding. They look like little soldiers trooping through the halls like that and it's so not childlike. There has to be other ways to help kindergarteners remember to be in a straight, quiet line without going full **KINDERGARTEN COP** on them. And with that I notice I'm atop my soapbox and I climb back down.

I walk to the side of my class, in the middle. This allows me to see the front and back clearly. I don't need to be in the front because my kids know where to go, and I don't like being in the back because then it's hard to see or get to the front. My student teacher will lead the line for the first little bit of the year. This helps them get the lay of the land and figure out the proper walking pace for a classroom. One that won't drag on forever but also won't leave anyone behind. In short order my student teacher will take my place in the middle and I will fall to the back so that I'm able to watch the student teacher and the class. I have my classroom of one and my classroom of students to watch.

Seating Chart

One of my personal favorite student teacher jobs is the seating chart. Full disclosure- I despise seating charts and use them as rarely as possible. I've spent my career teaching upper elementary, that's third, fourth, fifth, and sixth. By these ages I believe students should be able to choose their own seats. You should see (and will, if you follow this philosophy) their minds get blown when they walk in on the first day with their parents or guardians and timidly ask, "Where's my seat?" and you respond, "Pick one. You're a fifth grader. I don't need to tell you where to sit." Setting the stage, right here and now, for student choice and voice in my classroom. I will go on to clarify that I have final say and if I notice seating choices that are not working out I will move students, but on a case-by-case basis. A student of mine gave me a lovely portmanteau for this- smartnerships, a combination of smart and partnerships. It was one of those moments where I had to stop and collect myself and then tell the student, "Congratulations, you've just coined a term I'm going to use forever." The mini-moral here is it's ok to let students call out sometimes, because they're funny and clever. I'll now often tell kids to make smartnerships and find smartners, whether their choosing seats or making groups for project.

Maybe you teach smaller kids, or maybe you like having a seating chart. Or maybe, like me, you started out seating chart-free but because of classwide choices you decided a change had to be made and for a while implemented a seating chart. I'm not judging your seating choices, I'm asking that you think about the reasons behind the choices out loud before making a student teacher go along with them.

Mentor teachers- there are few things more fun than watching your student teacher try to devise a workable seating chart. Nothing crystallizes the inherent conflicts and difficulties of teaching a large number of unique individuals like trying to figure out who sits where. Seating charts, when I do have to do them, are a least favorite thing. They're also a great learning opportunity. So I give my student teacher the pleasure. Then I get to work on something else and surreptitiously watch as she slowly loses her mind.

"I'll put him here, her here, him here, her and her here, him other there, him over- no, he needs to be in the front, it's in his IEP. Ok, I'll switch him and her and now, oh, now she's next to him and they can't be near each other. I need a new piece of paper. Ok, this time I'll start with all the kids who need specific seating....I'm out of seats. I don't understand. I know, I'll move- no. Wait- no. Ok, instead of groups of four what if I do groups of six and one group of three and one group of two and, can I put someone alone? No. Hrm. Do you have another eraser? And can I put a kid in the hall because I'm out of space?"

It's fantastic.

8. What's Your Story Part 1

Student teaching is a singular experience, unique to each person who goes through the process. With this in mind, I reached out to a few wonderful educators from all levels and asked them to share a story or piece of advice gleaned from their time. The stories are uncut, and I have not added my own commentary. The reason for this is, I believe the stories speak for themselves, and I want you, the smart, savvy reader, to draw your own conclusions and learn your own lessons. That will be more powerful than anything I could add.

Jose Vilson- middle school math

To those who start education conversations with "Let's blame schools of ed," I'd say, "What a time to be alive."

By no means do I believe schools of education are perfect, but there's palpable progress in the way of discussing what's necessary for future teachers that I didn't feel during my time as a student teacher. In the way of equity, we didn't have *that* conversation until we forced it into our classes. The idea that our questions on intersectionality needed to hold space in the center of our pedagogy didn't exist. If anything, we got about half a session on disability (and it was awesome), but then it was back to procedures and theory.

As an NYC Teaching Fellow, my experience had multiple scaffolds that worth unpacking. The first was that the program designated my cohort to start two weeks early to relearn seventh through twelfth-grade math. I was only two years removed from passing Calculus 3, so it should have been a breeze. Those two years made enough of a difference to render my secondary math skills moot. I did the working hard thing and got my math credentials. From there, my cohort was integrated with the rest of the program in learning how to teach.

We have five weeks to get in teaching shape. That's four days a week of summer school teaching followed by grad school classes. On the Fridays where we weren't in front of kids, we sat through district presentations that mattered legally, but pedagogically would have made Paulo Freire weep. I spent Sunday through Thursday thoroughly preparing for this onerous and honorific task of teaching the most underserved kids.

It's easy to call these experiences bad. Chaotic, complicated, and predictable are more precise in the grand scope of things. Unlike the ludicrous stories that education reform tells, the teacher pipeline can't ever be squeaky clean so long as our society has racial, gender, religious, ability, and economic disparities as integral to its institutions. Summer school gave many of us a bitter taste for these disparities. It's easy to tell stories about our kids. Kids who let condoms and cigarettes spill from their pockets while reaching for their pencils. Kids who get too close to your personal stuff, but, upon interrogation, never know where it disappeared. Kids who love you one day, hate you the next. The adults who hone in on any of these flaws do so because of their own flaws. Adults who don't see the kids as kids. It might be appropriate to call them students here, but they're burgeoning human beings. I learned eventually that this is not a meant of minimizing their existence, but to grant them the full childhood they're often stripped of as children.

Unfortunately, the culture of the classrooms we were student teaching in wasn't reflected in my graduate classes. In the evening, we focused so much on *math* teaching that we didn't really talk about math *teaching*. One veteran Black teacher turned associate professor tried to develop scenarios only to have white students from fancy Ivy Leagues openly rebel against him, saying he didn't know any better and diminishing any chance we could tap into his wealth of knowledge. Alas. Our fellows leader, an older white gentleman, gave our cohort opportunities to discuss lesson planning, but he had a room that was half white and half of color. We all tiptoed around the race issue as to not offend.

With only a week or so left in class, I took affirmative action.

In one of our sessions, a white peer kept fumbling over the n-word. I looked around and noticed the anxiety from the white peers in the room, and disgust from the peers of color. I raised my hand and said, "Excuse me. Can I just close this door and ask people to just speak freely? If you need to use the n-word directly, just go ahead because the kids are gonna use it, and if we don't talk about race right now, it's gonna be a mess." I probably should have had a huddle with my peers before making such an executive decision, but … d'oh.

Maybe I should have kept the doors open. It shouldn't have been a secret.

From there, I noticed that the peers of color perked up because, for once, we were gonna talk from our Asian-Latinx-Black perspectives and our white peers would have to hear our stories outright. That worked for 15 minutes. But, as they were wont to do, the white facilitator and white peers started to shut down. After we opened the doors, the conversation never came up against until a few days later, when my fellows leader pulled me aside and said, "You really don't think we discuss race?"

I wanted to tell him, "Hell naw!" But the broke and tired student teacher told him "We got work to do, man."

Surely, there've been people that have asked schools of ed to discuss equality/equity for decades. My forefathers in this work have gone keep in the work, and for that, we must be thankful. Education culture is now at a precipice where *more* people have a fundamental understanding of why we must center these issues in preparing educators. But we have so much further to go before we can keep the doors open and onlookers won't flinch.

Shana White- K-12 Health and Physical Education

Physical education is one of those fields that does not receive a lot of love or respect. Honestly, understanding the human body, how the body functions, and movement patterns is hard. Background knowledge for physical education and health is its own form of STEM (Science Technology Engineering Math). Science of body, technical advancements of the health field, and the engineering and math principles involved with body movement, striking movements, and strategies with sports. On top of the depth of knowledge required for physical education, imagine then developing and/or executing curriculum that is age appropriate. Health and physical education as a field should be more respected and applauded than it is.

With the uniqueness of the expectations for a physical education/health teacher, my student teaching experience was extremely unique. When having conversations with colleagues, my student teaching experience left much to be desired. My undergrad degree covered the complete understanding of the human body (Health and Exercise Science), so when I decided to become a physical education teacher, I hoped my master's program would cover pedagogy, instructional practices and give me an opportunity to exercise what I learned in a classroom with teacher. While I did receive some instruction on pedagogy in the PE classroom and instructional strategies, I did not receive a legit opportunity to student teach. I was only provided one week during my two year program to work with students in a classroom setting. I had the opportunity in my Adaptive PE course to work with special education students for a week. As a class (there were less than 10 of us) we developed lesson plans to implement with the students that week. We had our twelve students come to campus and we taught them for thirty minutes. We worked on fitness, movement and small game activities during the week. While the experience was extremely valuable and helped me reaffirm my decision to enter the profession, it did not adequately prepare me for being responsible for a group of students daily. Only working with a group of twelve students with approximately ten other adults for a week is nowhere near adequate preparation for a full time health/physical education teacher. There was no preparation for things I dealt with my first few years teaching: classroom management, large class size, class engagement, class disruptions, and long term lesson planning. My time in the classroom over the past 12 years, I've been able to learn and adapt to the things I did not learn in a traditional student teaching program, but I always wonder how my career would have been with a traditional student teaching experience.

Megan Schmidt- High school math teacher

It was late January, 2004, Roosevelt Middle School* in Southeast Minneapolis: My first day of student teaching. Two buses, a light rail, and 5 blocks later, I had arrived to Vivian Zimmerman's* 8th grade math classroom. A sea of unfamiliar, but curious faces looked up at me briefly but seemed to be used to the interruption of random classroom visitors. There was nothing unusual about my student teaching experience from an outside observer's point of view. But as April turned to May which flowed into June, I began to resent the teacher whose job was to guide and mentor me into my full-time teaching career.

Toward the middle of the semester, Mrs. Zimmerman announced that she was pregnant...with twins. At the time, I couldn't empathize with her situation, but as the weeks went on, I began to see her mood and attitude toward me and the students shift dramatically. The most memorable moment happened when she left me in charge of a class full of students for the entire hour while she attended a doctor appointment. The students were making collages for their graduation ceremony which consisted of cutting and pasting construction paper to a poster board so I'm sure she felt I was capable of facilitating the activity. When Mrs. Zimmerman walked back into the room, the radio was on, there was paper scraps on the desks and floor, and kids were talking, laughing and having a good time reminiscing about their years at Roosevelt. Mrs. Zimmerman said to me at the end of the day, in front of the homeroom students, that she was outraged at the chaotic state her classroom was in when she returned and had regretted putting me in charge.

I'm grateful for this student teaching experience because it taught me some very valuable lessons which help me through some tough days, even 13 years later. First, always talk to coworkers with respect and professionalism, especially in front of the students. Second, what looks like chaos initially might actually be engagement and relationship building. Don't mistake noise and mess for a classroom void of learning. I still see Mrs. Zimmerman from time to time at math conferences and events. I give her a smile and a polite hello because I'm sure she did the best she could given her circumstances. I'm grateful, however, that I have the chance to do it differently with my own students.

Scott Bedley- 5th grade

It seems like it was yesterday. I'd never really stood in front of a class of students in a formal setting to give a lesson, although I had worked with kids for years at camps and in youth groups. My task was to teach cursive letter writing to an awesome group of 3rd graders. To put this in perspective, I was the kid who always had report card comments and teacher feedback that read something like "Your content is great but your penmanship (pre-word processing) is horrible," or at least that's what the words felt like to me. After getting the class excited about learning to write the letter "D" in cursive, I stepped to the board to model its formation for the kids. It was after just one letter demonstration that my "master teacher" stopped me by walking up front next to me and saying with one of those irritated smiles on her face and an equally "happy" irritated tone in her voice "I'm sorry boys and girls, Mr. Bedley isn't really good at teaching. You can go sit down now, Mr. Bedley." I was a bit in shock, deeply embarrassed and after a few minutes of reflecting on what had just happened, ready to quit teaching before I had even really started. Although I may have deserved the criticism, it was brutal to be embarrassed in front of the students in that way in my first shot. Later that day and with tears in my eyes, I met in the principal's office with both the principal Ron Moreland (a great friend to this day) and an amazing mentor Don Urger (who we lost to cancer later the next year) believing I wasn't cracked up to be a teacher. After sharing what had happened, and with encouraging words (along with a change of master teachers), I stayed. It was the moment I learned to take failures and harsh situations and use them to drive me to be the best I can be at my craft. Total transparency, I'm still self-conscious about handwriting anything in front of others but I use this story to help teach my students how they can turn failure into determination and a driving force to succeed.

Knikole Taylor- Blended Learning Specialist

Everyone needs a coach, someone on the sidelines telling cheering them on as they work towards their goals. There is no greater feeling than to have someone in our corner to turn to when things are hard or we simply need a listening ear. This is especially true for new teachers. During the first year in the classroom, there are many ups, downs, highs, and lows for brand new educators, and having someone to guide them and coach them through the process is priceless.

As a first year teacher, I was fortunate to have my father, a veteran educator turned administrator at the time, as my coach. His guidance and expertise with children and elementary mathematics were my lifeline. Not only did I not have any teaching experience, but I was also participating in an alternative certification program and had no formal training to be a teacher. Talk about someone who needed all of the help possible. I can still remember calling my dad a few weeks before my college graduation to tell him about my first job. I was excited, but he was elated to have his daughter follow in his footsteps and immediately began giving me advice on what to buy, what to do, and what to expect as a new teacher. As I rushed to the store to buy all of the cute letters and laminated posters, he encouraged me to not go overboard. He guided me to decorate my room without clutter, leaving room for student work and told me some students are unable to concentrate with wall to wall "stuff", a lesson I still hold to this day when I decorate any classroom or office space. Less is more. Once I was all set up in my classroom, a few weeks before school started, my dad and I began to set up meeting times to prepare for my students. Each and every single Saturday morning, my new husband and I would gather all of my teaching materials which included my scope and sequence, teacher editions, student textbooks, my laptop, and whatever I thought I wanted to use with students loaded up in multiple bags. My dad and I would sit down together at his kitchen table for hours going day by day to ensure I had a plan of action. He would first go over the math to make sure his daughter, an honors math student with a degree in finance, understood what she was teaching. At the time, I really thought he simply enjoyed having someone to "teach" each weekend because clearly, I knew fifth grade mathematics. However, as the weeks progressed, I realized the importance of combining tough standards to ensure I understood exactly what students should know. He would ask me probing questions like, "Kniki, what will you do if the kids don't do this?" or "If a kid says this as the answer, what does that mean?" I can remember him laughing as I would write things down word for word, as if I were preparing a script for my classroom. I hung on his every word and still use many of his strategies and guiding questions with the teachers and students I support today. Those weekends were my lifeline, my guidebook to ensure I was able to give students my best daily. I would pick his brain about lessons to use outside of the textbook and classroom management issues because I knew early on that I didn't like a book and students needed more. He would give me feedback and advice and be my sounding board. Those mentoring sessions that lasted all day and sometimes into the night were invaluable and propelled me to become the team lead for fifth grade the following year. More importantly, the enabled me to go into my classroom each day with confidence, prepared to give my students my best and meet their needs.

9. Pet Peeves and Weak Links

Pet Peeves

Tattletales drive me up the wall. A whiny tone of voice makes me cringe. A well-placed eye-roll requires a ten-count and some breathing. It's important to know what your buttons are because the kids in your classes will find all of them. They'll push them over and over again. On accident for the most part, so you'll need to learn not to take things personally. It's kids testing out their world. They'll do it on purpose too, because it's instructive to see what kind of control you can have over an adult.

Before you step into a classroom it's important to take some self-evaluation time and honestly chart out what makes your teeth grind. Don't pretend that when you become a teacher all those human parts of you go away. Don't fool yourself into thinking that the care you feel for these children will drown out the things that have bothered you for your entire life. You're still a human. Being a teacher doesn't remove that part of you. In fact, I'd forever argue that the more human you are, the better teacher you are.

Kids don't want a robot teacher. They want someone they can identify with and see themselves in. They want you to be flesh and blood, because then you'll laugh with them and cry with them. Oh yes, you will cry with them. If you do any read-alouds with your class you're going to cry, because children's book authors are the most terrible people ever. E.B. White is going to make you sit in front of your class and read, "No one was with her when she died," from chapter 23 of *Charlotte's Web* and you will cry. You'll read about Little Ann dying of a broken heart in *Where the Red Fern Grows* and you will cry. You'll read about Stella dying in *The One and Only Ivan* and you'll cry. You'll cry when Leslie falls off the rope in *Bridge to Terabithia.* Let yourself. Man teachers- I'm especially talking to you because it's important our boys (and girls) see that it's ok to feel emotions other than anger. We're the front line of breaking down things like toxic masculinity. If you're lucky enough to be a man teacher, especially but not limited to the elementary level, you've got a very special opportunity to be a role model that can change things for the better and move us all forward. No pressure.

Mentor teachers- you know your pet peeves when it comes to your students. But what about with other adults? What are the things that kids will do that roll off your back that, if done by an adult, will feel like an icepick to the eye socket?

It turns out I'm a stickler for punctuality in grown-ups. Most kids have no control over when they get to school. There are some who are completely independent in the morning because mom, dad, guardian, whoever works early or late so it's on the kid to wake up, get ready, and get to the bus. I suppose their tardiness is their own fault, but they've got so much going on in that case that it's hard to hold it against them. Please remember that nothing in school happens in a vacuum. Most of our kids are woken up, spurred along, and dropped off at school or the bus stop by the adult they live with. "Mom overslept," is a legitimate excuse for being late. As a heads-up student teachers, so is, "Our house burned down and we're living in a hotel," or, "We had to move because our landlord kicked us out and now we're driving here from across town," and dozens more. If a student is late, it's not their fault. We can encourage them to encourage mom or whoever to get them to school on time, but that's it. Keep your priorities in order.

Adults who are late, that's a horse of a different color. I know the struggle, student teachers. I'm not a morning person. I especially wasn't a morning person when I started my own student teaching program. This was in the BeforeTimes, before cell phones were in everyone's pocket and a mentor teacher was a text message away. If I was late waking up, not as rare an occurrence as I wish I could say, my only choice was to make like a bread truck and haul buns. There were several Serious Conversations between myself and my first mentor teacher before I learned how to set multiple alarms, a practice I continue to this day because I live in fear of waking up, looking at the time, and realizing that the time on my phone is also the time the bell rings at school. It's not a joke or hyperbole when a teacher tells you they've woken up, misread the time with blurry eyes, and been halfway out the door before their brain catches up. I've been in the middle of making myself lunch before thinking, "Why am I still so very tired? Why is it so dark? Why does the oven clock say 3:12? ...oh. Right." Good luck getting back to sleep, by the way. Still, that's better than being late. Even if it does then cascade into waking up every thirty minutes because now you don't trust yourself to wake up properly.

What I'm saying, student teachers, is get to bed on time and set a few alarms. And maybe invest in a coffee maker.

In a coincidental twist, I learned that tardiness by adults bothers me by being on the other side of the mentor teacher/student teacher relationship. My second student teacher rolled in late a few days in a row. Each day I said, "You need to be here at this time. You can't keep being late." Like me, he was genuinely apologetic. Like me, he was late again. Mentor teachers- it's up to you how you handle this. You don't want to threaten or fly off the handle. You don't want to destroy the relationship. We're here to help. What I did say was, "Dude. I don't want to be a jerk about this. Please don't make me." That was enough. He was never late again. I'm not a nut, I know that traffic can be unpredictable and sometimes kids or cars refuse to cooperate. As with the students in my classroom, I'm flexible and understanding with my student teachers. To a point.

Mentor teachers- once you understand what those pet peeves of yours are, you need to communicate them. The best way to wreck your classroom environment is to be inconsistent with your students, right? To enforce rules the kids didn't know were rules. The same goes for your classroom of one. Talk to your student teachers openly and honestly. "These are the things that will bug the heck out of me." (Full disclosure, unless my student teacher specifically asks me to not curse when it's just the two of us, there's zero chance the word I'll use is 'heck'.) But, like all things educational, we still shouldn't be drawing hardlines. "These are the things that bug the heck out of me," shouldn't be followed with, "...so never do them ever not even once or so help me." Everything is a dialogue. It's all a conversation. It's a year-long relationship. Once again, keep the power dynamic in mind. Mentor teachers hold all the power here. In theory we could say, "Never do this thing," and the student teacher will need to jump through that hoop. But there's only so many hoops we can put in front of someone before they get resentful and tired of jumping.

Student teachers- you are allowed to say the same thing to your mentor teacher. We are here to help you, so you need to outline any deal breakers. I made a joke in the previous paragraph about my use of adult language in adult company, and it's completely true. It's also a First Conversation topic for me. "When it's just us I have a tendency to be informal with my language. I'll never do it in front of the kids, but in general conversation I will. If that makes you uncomfortable tell me now and I'll curb it."

The language thing also lends an air of informality to the student teacher/mentor teacher relationship, which I value. I'm not good at formality. This is another conversation we'll have early. With our students we are supposed to be friendly but not friends. There's a defined line in that relationship that should be maintained for professional reasons. In my classroom of one, I've found it helps to be friends. It's not a must. But by the end of the year we will be more co-teachers than student teacher/mentor teacher, and a friendly bent to the relationship will make the co-teaching easier and more fun. Think about the classroom environment. When the teachers are having fun and are relaxed, the students are having fun and feel relaxed. When a classroom is relaxed information passes more easily through it. Being honest with what makes you human makes all of that more possible.

Weak Links

Much like there are places student teachers and mentor teachers will naturally clash personality-wise, there are also places where teaching styles don't mesh. It's not the job of a mentor teacher to force a student teacher into a box. That's not beneficial. Why? Say it with me- **A mentor teacher's job is to prepare the student teacher to be successful in their own classroom on Day One.** Dictating that Thou Must Teach Like Thine Own Mentor Teacher does not do that.

Plus *glances around and whispers*, I'm better at teaching some subjects than others. I know, I know. You're saying, "But Doug, you're writing an education book for teachers. Surely you are a master of the art! Stop being so modest." Would that I could, dear reader. But it's not modesty. It's honesty. If I truly want to prepare my student teacher for a classroom of his or her own, I must force them out of my nest and into the world.

Like honestly evaluating pet peeves, a mentor teacher must also honestly evaluate the subjects and aspects of teaching where they lack. It does no one any good for a mentor teacher to focus only on their strengths. I, for instance, am capable of coming up with creative, different, and varied language arts lessons. I can integrate all kinds of things, from making to robotics to technology to science and social studies, into projects. What I'm not great in is being creative in my math lessons. That's not to say I don't try. Every conference I go to I hunt down the math sessions to make myself better. It feels great to go to a session about edtech and nod along, knowing what the presenter is talking about and where they're going, but it makes me a better teacher to go to a session on math instruction and furrow my brow and take pages of notes.

I'm also not great at data collection. I have specific opinions about grades in elementary school that translate into me spending less time on grading than other teachers. However, being as grades are important in the system we're working within, I have to make sure my student teachers see a multiple of ways to assess and record information. Grades are important in that schools and districts think they're important, and parents have been trained by experience to feel they're important. Students put emphasis on what you as the teacher act like is important. I focus on the learning rather than the grading, and as such students rarely ask me what their grades are. They should know how they're doing and how they've grown. We should have discussed it. That's good enough. Grades aren't going anywhere, but they shouldn't motivate your students.

As long as I'm baring my weaknesses, since it's important to be an example, I also struggle mightily with organization. I'm a piler. I will clean my desk with the intention of keeping it clean and neat, like the teachers across the hall and next door. But invariably the piles grow. Every teacher evaluation I've ever had has looked good in every category except Organization. That one normally has some kind of suggestion next to it to find a place for everything. Students will sometimes give me the side-eye when I tell them their desk is a mess. I do what I can. It's organized enough. It works for me. I'm not trying to change that because it's part of my process. Kids don't get away with it yet because they don't have a process yet and I hate finding old sandwiches buried under last week's work.

However, piling might not be part of my student teacher's process. I would be remiss if I didn't do everything I could to shore up the weaknesses I might be passing on, organizational, data-wise, or otherwise. It's my job as a mentor teacher to ask around and see if my student teacher might be able to watch other teachers do their thing. Student teachers- ask to see other classrooms anyway, it's good for you. Mentor teachers- we know who the rock star math teachers are at school. If that's a place where you know you could be a better model, model getting better at something without ego and seek to send your student teacher to other rooms for short periods of time. Find the teachers at your school that are great at what you're not, and ask them, "Pretty please I'll buy you a coffee, can my student teacher hang out in your room, watch you, and then pick your brain?" This is devious and self-serving, by the way, because then the student teacher comes back with new ideas and gets to teach me, the mentor teacher. Flip the relationship at any opportunity. Students should never see us as the Fount of All Knowledge. Student teachers should learn early that education is a team sport.

I can't resist digging into that metaphor to explain it fully. Education is not a team sport like football or hockey. In the lower grades it's a team sport like swimming is a team sport. We train together, but we work alone. We strengthen each other in practice and the result comes from a collective effort, but when it comes to a relay race there isn't actual teamwork happening. Each person's individual effort, one at a time, creates a successful whole. The upper grades, middle and high school, when teachers are sharing students, then it's a team sport like baseball. Everyone has their own job, their own place. The teachers need to pay attention to what's happening to the ball, but the main effort come when the ball is hit their way.

Kindergarten is like four and five year olds playing soccer. It's a mess and I have no idea how anyone knows what's going on, but they do look like they're having fun.

Without honest reflection none of this works. You can get through a school year by yourself without reflecting, but your students won't get the best you. You could be a mentor teacher without reflecting, but then your student teacher is being cheated and you're missing out on one of the most valuable parts of the process. Over the course of the year, both mentor teacher and student teacher should grow and change. They should work together to do that.

It's a relationship, and that requires the ultimate in open communication and honest assessment to be fulfilling.

Doug Robertson

10. Digital Naïveté

If you've been in education as a teacher or as a education student for any length of time you have heard the term "digital native." It appears in such sentences as, "Kids today are digital natives. They know how to use technology because it's around. You hand a two year old an iPad and he can open apps and play games." First of all, ignore anyone who seriously starts a sentence with, "Kids today." This person is drawing arbitrary lines in shifting sands to fit a narrative which exists only in their head. Secondly, if there was such a thing as a digital native, which there isn't, this is the worst evidence to use to convince an educator.

"You have a two year old with an iPad and he can open apps and start playing with it." What part of that sentence tickles your teacher brain and makes you think that means kids can just simply learn using technology? How is the ability to use the most basic aspect of a purposefully user-friendly tool evidence that kids born in a certain generation exist in this world where they're capable of using and learning with technology naturally. That's why the word native is there, it suggests that this is the world they live in, so it's the world they're automatically able to interact effectively with. Putting aside for a moment the socio-economic implications of such a statement because, woo, think about who is centered in that scenario, let's think about other tools that are user-friendly and the assumptions that could be made the same way. This is like handing someone a saw and a piece of wood and, after they cut the wood in half, declaring, "This person is a sawing native! Now build me a house." The most basic understanding of a tool is not an indication of a natural ability to use it to create, learn, or grow. It means the designers made a good product for the general public.

Student teachers- blanket statements run wild in education. Yes, I know that was a blanket statement about blanket statements. "Kids today," is always the start of a blanket statement. Be suspicious. Be wary. Keep an eye out for of easy solutions and generalities. Education is a lot of things, but easily done isn't one of them. "Kids today," also assumes that every child comes from a background where technology is around and available. Technology is the next great socio-economic divide. Access to the internet is not as universal as you might think. Huge chunks of rural America are still struggling to be connected. Data plan costs restrict how much internet usage families get. In parent-teacher conferences I'll ask families what their connectivity is like. More parents than you might imagine will raise their phones and say, "This is it." They don't have wifi or laptops. They've got a phone plan. This makes me think hard about the kinds of technology-based projects I might send home. Digital natives are a myth.

The same technological divide goes for schools. You might get lucky and end up in a placement with 1:1 technology. This means that each and every student has a tablet or computer. You might also end up in a classroom with two laptops that are about fifteen minutes removed from being typewriters. Desktop computers with hard drive towers that you need to crank to get started. A VHS player. You might end up with a mentor teacher who knows how to use a computer to help students learn, or you might end up with one that knows how to email and that's about it.

Mentor teachers- that's on us. It's getting harder and harder to accept that there are some teachers who don't know how to use a variety of technologies in their classrooms to promote and support learning. I'm not talking about pre-paid websites and programs that are supposed to do all the teaching for us. That's not using technology to promote and support learning, that's moving from paper worksheets to digital worksheets. It's still a worksheet, it's still teacher-centered, and it's still boring. I'm talking about content creation tools, deep-dive investigation tools, tools that are changing and improving as we speak, but take time to learn.

While every teacher should be technologically literate, it is especially true that mentor teachers need to be caught up. It's our job to be guiding student teachers into the future of education, not helping them maintain the past. In the previous chapter I talked about knowing your weaknesses and shoring them up so as to best help your student teacher. If you're weak in classroom technology get thee to some edtech conferences. Beginner, intermediate, expert, there's sessions for everyone out there now. Take responsibility for the preparation of both your students and your student teacher and fill out all aspects of their education by filling out all aspects of your own.

Student teachers will be coming to us with possibly more technology know-how than we have, but without the pedagogical background to make use of it. This is another chance for the student to become the master and to teach their mentor teacher how to do something. Let your students see your student teacher teaching you. It reinforces the truth that the student teacher is a teacher to them, and it models being a learner no matter your age or position. Student teachers- do not be shy about this. If you know of a website, program, or trick that you think will enhance a lesson, shout it out. You can even hedge your bet, shout it out with, "I know this is a thing. I think we can use it. I don't know how." That's great. It means you and your mentor teacher can build something new together through investigation and discovery.

Digital citizenship is a phrase that gets thrown around quite a bit, and it's another that I have issue with. Not because it's wrong, like digital native, but because I think it's too long. Digital citizenship is really just citizenship. It's all about being a good person. There are some who would add to that, "online and in real life," but who you are online is who you are. Period. It is real life. We can't pretend that a person's online persona is not in some way attached to who they actually are. As we live more and more of our lives on the internet, this will only become more true. I have students with all manner of social media profiles that, in theory, have an age gate. I can tell them, "No! No, you cannot be there. Delete your account and we shall never speak of this again." Or I can be a teacher and help them navigate the fun and dangerous waters of the internet. This goes for both student teachers and mentor teachers. Student teachers- the kids might even look to you more for this kind of thing because the mentor teacher is an Old and Olds don't get it.

Teach them digital footprint is a misnomer too. Digital tattoo is more correct. The internet never forgets and things you think are deleted may still exist.

Citizenship means teaching kids to talk online like they know there's a real person on the other end. It means working towards making the internet a better world too.

While we're here, student teachers- be smart about your own

online presence once you're in a classroom. Make yourself harder to find, lockdown who can friend request you, protect yourself. Many teachers will create two accounts, a personal one and a professional one. I'm of two minds about this. On one hand, districts don't yet know how to handle the difference between what happens online and what happens at work. Personally, I don't believe an employer should punish someone for what they post online unless it's directly abusive or terrible. If you're online posting racist comments or Nazi memes, yeah, you don't get to work with kids anymore. But you shouldn't be punished for who you are unless who you are is a jerk. More important than whether or not you might get in trouble with the boss, however, is what if the kids see what you're posting? This is where making yourself harder to find is good idea. Right now, as you read this, you might shrug. Wait until a kid walks up to you one morning and says, "Looks like you have a fun weekend." Be aware.

Back in the classroom, technology's greatest use is not making things easier. It's making things more connected and expanding the ability of students to create. Computers will let you show your students things you never thought you could. It could be simple. "We're reading about the Statue of Liberty so here's a 360 degree view of it. Now you find me three facts about the Statue you think are interesting." That's still basic research though. You could have done that with a book, just not as quickly. Push the envelope and use the technology to find ways to make students create rather than consume. That's real learning, the taking of information and transforming it in some way. Could your students create their own tour of the State of Liberty? Could they use a green screen and a phone to make a documentary? Could you find a 3D design program and let them build their own Statue of Liberty, or let them rebuild the State of Liberty as though it were gifted now rather than in 1875? The answer to all of those is yes, and there's a million more things your students could do. If you let them.

This brings us all the way back to the technology as a tool, like a saw. Described above is asking students to build a house (or a Statue of Liberty) with that tool. They will need some basic understanding of the tool in order to do that. Here again you have a choice- what kind of a teacher will you be? Will you take the pencil from the child's hand and show him how to draw that shape, or will you stand at his shoulder and watch, offering advice as asked? My favorite way to introduce a new technology tool is to present it to students and let them play with it for a while. No goals, just pushing buttons and seeing what happens. Then I challenge them to Make a Thing. I leave it broad. It's investigation and exploration. Sometimes, instead of asking them to Make a Thing I'll ask them to Break a Thing, like a website I made or a slideshow or some code. The only thing more motivating and freeing than being given the chance to create is the chance to destroy. Adults never tell you to destroy something. Between you and me, taking something apart is a great way to learn how it works. Plus, the students don't know this, but after they take it apart I am going to ask them to put it back together so it works. Alternatively, I could ask them to take the pieces and make something completely new. Let them explore. Then, let them share with each other what they learned. It will warm you teacher heart to hear, "Hey, come here, check this out! Look what I figured out." Plus, they'll figure out how to do things you don't know how to do and they'll teach you.

CLARIFICATION: There are those tech integrators who

claim, "The students will learn it first and they can teach you how to use it." That's not what I'm saying. Your students should not be giving you the baseline knowledge. They should be giving you Small Rocks. The exploration allows students to find their own Big Rocks, but you still need a plan. You're still the teacher. At the end of the exploration there should be a project, a goal. "Take what you've learned and build something that uses all those skills." Teach them one specific skill and ask them to find ways to use it. You can't step all the way back, then you're not the teacher at all, you're just a person in the classroom. Like everything else in education, it's all about balance. Don't take the pencil out of the child's hands, but don't trust that they'll puzzle it out for themselves. You're there for a reason. You went to school for a reason. Teach your students to learn through exploration in an efficient manner.

Technology also makes the world a smaller place. This is in no way an new idea, but it has remarkable echoes and implications for a classroom. I put together a Read Across America program a few year ago that ignored the America part. I reached out to friends across the globe and brought them into my classroom through the magic of video-chatting to read to my students. A friend living and teaching in the Middle East blew my kids' minds when he told them that it was 2am tomorrow where he was. "What? No no, it's Thursday here, what do you mean it's Friday there?" Instant geography lesson, student-driven, because when a kid's mind is blown she will find ways to understand that feeling. One year I was sent a Day In The Life video from a teacher in Ghana. Students in Oregon have no concept of what life is like in New York, let alone Ghana. I had no concept of what life is like in Ghana until that video. In return we made a

Day In The Life video too. Student-driven, they helped me figure out what to film and how to cut it together. We used a video from somewhere else to better understand an unfamiliar culture, and then to better understand ourselves.

Students can share their writing with students around the world. Turning something in to the teacher is fine, but it's not terribly motivating. Posting something online where other kids might see it? That's motivating. Then they'll care about spelling and grammar in ways that me saying, "You should care about spelling and grammar," simply can't match. They'll excitedly read what other students are writing and when you've got a kid who won't read what you've got on offer in class excited about reading what another kid wrote, that's a win. That's an in. That's technology improving your teaching.

The world of an elementary school student is small. Part of becoming good citizens is students starting to see themselves as global citizens. To understand the plights and struggles of people who aren't like them. Lip service to the Civil Rights movement doesn't do anything. Spending a month pretending Black History isn't America History so its entirety should be contained in the shortest month of the year doesn't do anything. Using technology to make that real, make the people impacted real, that's important. You will have students who are impacted by racism, sexism, homophobia. Students silenced or cowed. Your classroom will, of course, be a safe, accepting place for those kids. If it won't be, please put this book down, tender your resignation, get back into your time machine, and enjoy the 1940s. Technology is a way for those kids to share their stories and feel as though their voices have value beyond the walls of your room.

Mentor teachers and student teachers- there are a million reasons for you to get good at and comfortable using technology in your classrooms. It will help your kids, strengthen you pedagogically, and assure that you're constantly moving forward instead of backwards. Technology is only a tool, it cannot do any of those things by itself. A computer is only as smart as the person using it. I try to keep this in mind when I'm ready to put my forehead through my laptop for not doing what I *know* I'm telling it to do.

Student teachers- if you need one more reason to find ways to use technology in your classrooms, let this be it: It'll get you jobs. Districts and principals aren't looking for new hires with the same old skills. They're looking for people who will be leaders, guiding the school into the future of educational technology. Come to job interviews with a website resume ready to show them and a digital portfolio full of videos, images, and a variety of other multimedia things you and your students did during your time student teaching and you'll get to choose where you work.

Technology is a place where the mentor teacher/student teacher relationship can easily flip. Let it. Let it be liquid, changing shape, flexible. Learn from each other and in that way get stronger together. For yourselves. For your students, today and forever forward.

11. They Didn't Teach Me This In Teacher School

Based on the title, you should be able to tell this is a chapter aimed more at student teachers, but, as I wrote at the start of the book, this is a holistic practice.

Universities work so very hard to prepare student teachers for teaching. Years of classes, dozens and dozens of credit-hours. How to look at data. What educational theories are in vogue and which are passé. Research, research, research. They try to give student teachers as many tools as possible so that when they step into a classroom they're ready to teach.

Then a student looks up at you and says, "Can you help me write a letter to my dad? He's in prison."

Where was that class? Did you miss it? Did you skip the day they talked about all the things kids will say and do that you will be completely unprepared for? No, the university never covered that because there are things that can't be communicated clearly enough in theory. Which is why you don't know what day your program covered consoling a child who is crying inconsolably because her best friend, well her ex-best friend, got mad at her for using her purple marker again without asking and ripped her paper. "Like, ripped it in half?" you'll ask, trying to be reasonable and understand the situation. No, just a tiny rip in the corner. But you don't understand and now she hates her ex-best friend forever. Until you see them playing tetherball at recess later.

How did you handle the paper ripping? What were you taught in school? It's destruction of property. Of course, theft lead to the destruction of property. But two wrongs don't make a right, right? So to solve the problem you...Hmmm. Depends on on the age of the students. The real answer is students should be able to be guided into solving most interpersonal conflicts on their own. Even the littlest humans, at some point, can learn to solve problems without going straight to the teacher for everything.

You'll want to be Superman or Wonder Woman (or Captain America or Ms Marvel, depending on your affiliation). Your urge as an adult who has decided that No One Shall Be Bullied In My Class will be to swoop in and save the day, solve the problem, and dispense justice as you see fit.

No. No no no no.

No.

Thou art not a superhero. Take your, "I'm a teacher, what's you superpower?" mug and throw it away. You know what superheroes do? They solve problems and save people. You know what your students do not need? Someone to solve their problems and save them.

You are NOT there to save these kids. Get that out of your head right now. You're not there to solve their problems or fix them either. Never think about how you can "fix" a kid. Kids aren't broken. There is a ton of baggage that comes with the Savior Complex.

You can *help*. You can *guide*. That's our job.

It's like the old proverb says- *Give a student a solution to a problem, and you'll have a line of kids around your desk forever. Teach a student to solve their own problems, and you'll be free to help as needed.*

Heroism is so tempting. But who are we saving? The racial implications of who teachers normally are (there's a lot of white men and women out there in our ranks) and who we think needs saving are legion. Be aware. Be reflective.

I'm not saying you're not to care for your kids, worry about your kids, and do everything you can to help your kids, but you are not saving them. When we do our job the best, we are giving students the tools and opportunities to save themselves.

I hope you were taught that. And if not, now you know. It's a mindset that impacts your every interaction.

Bathroom Plan

There are plenty of other things you weren't taught in school. What's your bathroom plan? How well have you thought it through? Can you honestly tell me that you know the difference between a kid faking it and a kid whose teeth are floating? How many times is a kid allowed to leave the room during a lesson? Sometimes, if a bunch of kids are leaving it's because they're bored and it's on you. Occasionally, it's because it's after lunch and the basketball game was too good to ruin with something like leaving to pee. Do you know which is which?

Have your mentor teacher explain their bathroom plan, and explain why it's their bathroom plan. Err on the side of caution.

Human Growth and Development

This goes out specifically to my future man teachers in the upper grades- get comfortable with women's body processes. I teach fifth grade, and this is the age when some girls enter that wonderful time in their lives that signals they're becoming women. And it's incredibly embarrassing for many of them. Your job is understanding and empathy. I've had kids unable to say the words, "I have to go to the bathroom right now because I'm on my period," because holy jeeze it's hard to say that to their dad, let alone their man teacher. These are kids who like me and trust me. Sometimes mom will email me (always mom, haven't had a dad send this email yet) to let me know in case her daughter has to leave the room for any reason. Like I'm going to question a girl who gets that look on her face and earnestly asks for a break. I've had their friends try to explain to me why they're in the office, "Well, you see, she's um, she's got, uh, you know" *gestures generally towards area in question*. That's the brave friend, by the way. The one willing to fall on the grenade so her friend doesn't get in trouble for not coming back to class with everyone else. The fifth grade boys, by the way, have zero clue what is going on in these conversations. None. Which is a problem. One of my soapbox causes is that we should be teaching human growth and development for both genders to both genders. Yeah, it's real uncomfortable at first for them, but it's better than having another generation of boys growing up making ignorant period and PMS jokes. They should see each other as human, not as separate species.

Staying in the upper grades, both genders are going through changes. There will be smells, and you'll need to be diplomatic and scientific about dealing with those smells so everyone is comfortable. There will be hormones. Speaking as a fifth grade teacher, the kids who leave me at the start of winter break are not always the kids who come back after winter break. Growth happens fast, and there's a lot of pressure and confusion that comes with that. Empathy, understanding, and conversations with your mentor teacher will help you safely navigate these waters.

Heightened Situations

Kids get wound up. Many times, they still working through the developmental stages where they can self-calm or see past the immediate emotion. It's important not to question a child's impression of a situation. What he or she says he or she feels is a truth. The reaction we the teachers feel is warranted in response to whatever the stimulus is should be reflected on carefully before putting it out into the world. Telling a kid he's overreacting rarely works and teaches a student that he should not trust his own emotional responses to things. My current principal is a wonderful human and administrator, and not just because she lets me get away with all kinds of nonsense in my classroom. She understands the physiological reactions to stressors we have, and how we can help kids understand and work through those. She talks about how when we get upset and stressed and start to escalate all the blood rushes to the fight or flight centers of the brain, and these are not places from which a person can have a rational conversation. We've all felt it. Something triggers us and before you know it you're so pissed you can't think, but you can also almost see outside yourself enough to think, "I wish I could stop this." And once you have that realization you begin the process of de-escalation on your own. Children get like that too, and we have to teach them to calm themselves down in safe ways. Talk about recognizing the physical and emotional signs that they're getting worked up and finding ways to remove themselves from the situation, find a safe place, and come down to a place where talking it out is possible. You will have plans in place for these students, so they never feel trapped. Give them an out.

Do not escalate. I will write that. You will read it. But you won't really know what I mean by that until you're in it.

Did your university teach you how to deal with a kid who looks you in the eye, posits that you fornicate with your mother, and flips a desk? A kid who gets so upset that he scratches his arms until he bleeds because he doesn't know how else to deal with how he's feeling? By the way, that's somehow an improvement because he used to throw desks, so now at least he's the only one getting hurt instead of everyone. And the kid who writes in her journal that she wishes she were dead? You will see this. It's going to happen. Be prepared. Except, you can't really be.

Your heart is going to break for these students. You're going to feel guilty because in the midst of all the empathy you're feeling you'll also be thinking, "How am I going to teach this kid to multiply?" Hopefully your school has a counselor. An expert who you go to for help, because these things are well above your pay grade and training. Eventually you'll get on-the-job training working with these extreme examples, but it's better to have a team with you. All of these situations come with delicate conversations with parents and guardians. Conversations where you can accidentally accuse a parent of something without meaning it because you think you're upset by all this? You have no idea. Accept that you have no idea.

This is the part where I tell you exactly how to deal with all these situations. Except I can't. There's no all-encompassing trick to helping students through emotional turmoil except to crank your empathy up to eleven and remember that you're dealing with a child. It's not personal, it's not their fault. Work with the experts around you to give the child the tools and support needed to be successful not just in your class, but in life. Every single one of these situations will be unique. That's one of the best and hardest parts of teaching- there will never come a day when you know you've seen it all, because the second you think that, a child will throw down a situation that's brand new to you.

Bullying

What is bullying, anyway? It's a repeated taking of power from one person or group by another person or a group of other people. It happens physically and emotionally. It can come through kicking and punching, verbal barbs, or shunning. Pretending to solve it by telling a kid, "Sticks and stones, man," only resonates so much. Especially because we all know that saying is a lie, words hurt all the time.

Bullying or any other kind of aggressive behavior meant to make someone feel unsafe are things I will not tolerate in my classroom. My room should be and will be a safe place for everyone because it's our home. It's where we learn and grow together. It has to be safe or it doesn't work. It has to be safe because no one deserves feeling unsafe. You cannot assume students know what bullying is. They often think it's just being mean, but it's more than that. Bullying is a fairly narrow act that gets used to cover a broad array of things. I'm not saying you shouldn't deal with all the smaller abuses and microaggressions that will happen in your room, I am saying that words matter and bullying is a specific act. This is a conversation you have to have with your class. It's actually multiple conversations because it's not an easy issue and there's no simple fix.

Mentor teachers- this is a conversation you should have with your student teachers. You know what it looks like specifically in your area and age group, and you'll be better able to explain it. You'll also better be able to explain the specific school and district policies in place, because it's different everywhere.

Gossip

A favorite saying of a PE teacher I know is, "Gossip is like glitter, it's fun for a while, but then it gets on everything and it's impossible to get off." It depends on what grade you end up student teaching in, but chances are you'll get to experience the joy of gossip management.

Gossip isn't tattling, because it doesn't flow towards an authority figure. Gossips often do their level best to keep away from the teachers because they know, either because they've been taught or because they can just tell, the teacher would not be a fan of it.

Because it's important to be clear about what things are, and this is a conversation you'll have with your student teachers and your students, gossip is the spreading of rumors about someone by others without the knowledge or consent of the victim and regardless of the truth of the statements. It might seem innocuous, it might be true, or have seeds of truth, or it might be a total lie. No matter what it's bad, because it erodes the foundation of trust and safety your class should be built on. It could take the form of, "She likes him," but it also can look like, "She said that he said that I said that he said that she said." That looks like hyperbole. It's not. Student teachers- you'll be amazed at what kids will buy into when they haven't learned the interpersonal skill of staying out of it or parsing what's reasonable and what's wrong. Some kids will also magically always find themselves in the middle of gossip, with no idea how they got there. "I was just telling my friend they were talking about him." Like they're helping. All the time. Right in the middle. And still confused why you're pulling them aside again to have another talk about what is helping and what is spreading rumors. This is why whole class conversations are important. So everyone knows.

Gossiping can sometimes be accidental. As always, start

from a place of trust. Even with the kids that you think might not have earned it. That whole, "I act this way because it's the way they expect me to act," isn't just a trope in the movies. It's a real motivator that really happens to students. The best way to keep your troublemaker kids as troublemakers is to treat them like they're guilty all the time. Especially because there will be those time when they're actually innocent and then you are the jerk.

Gossip can be a form of bullying. It's easy and painless for the person starting it, and they can hide in the confusion of he said she said that you said I said. Oh what a tangled web we weave when we practice to mess with Steve.

Student teachers- you have a choice on how to deal with it, and again, lean on your mentor teachers. If it's not a big problem talk to the perpetrators. Individually. These aren't mobsters from movies, coordinating their stories to confuse the fuzz. These are kids who can't keep a story straight, who will sell their friends down the river, or who default to honesty because they all are good kids. The latter happens a lot, especially as they realize the former. Those one-on-one meetings take place with you taking notes. Then if you need to, you pull everyone involved together. Not for a Gotcha, but to make crystal clear that their stories did not line up and you know you're being lied to. Or you can have a whole class Come To Jesus conversation. At my school, we have Class Meeting scheduled for every other week, and that's the perfect time. Unless it's a big problem and needs to be dealt with earlier. Then lesson plans get pushed to the side so I can take care of the thing that will prevent learning from happening. Don't let problems fester. It's all about not pointing fingers, talking about the impact and how it makes people feel, and helping the kids find empathy. Class Meeting isn't for small, interpersonal problems. It's for Complaints, Questions, and Comments, the free sharing of thoughts using a Speaking Object of some kind. I have a small, stuffed Darth Vader because I am a nerd stereotype. No talking unless you're holding Lord Vader.

As wonderful as the internet is, it's a great venue for students to gossip and bully each other, and it's gray area for a lot of schools still. Administrations differ on how to deal with something that's happening from home, but is impacting school. I had a student who created a false Instagram account for another student, and then started posting all manner of ridiculousness on it. Others joined in with comments and jokes. The victim didn't even know what was happening until someone tagged her in it. Luckily, some of these kids aren't the most savvy of hackers and they were using their own accounts, so it was easy to track who said what with evidence. And, as I said before, they were more than willing to sell out the original culprit. We dealt with it by having conversations with the parents and having restorative discipline conversations between the students. Mentor teachers- we're still learning to deal with social media bullying as well, so it's a perfect chance to have a planning meeting with your administrator and student teacher together to hash out a response that is fair but effective. Student teachers- sitting in those meetings sounds really good in job interviews and gives you answers to interview questions other candidates won't have.

Tattling

Tattling is one of the most confounding things students will do because it puts the teachers in an awkward position. On one hand you want to take everyone's reports into consideration because you want to know what's happening in your room. On the other hand I really really don't need to know that he looked at you again. The biggest issue with tattling is when a student is trying to draw attention away from themselves by throwing their friend under the bus first. You rarely get the whole story from a tattle.

"He hit me."

"Why did he hit you?" Always ask why. As a general rule, for everything.

"I don't know." This will often be the response. You'll hear, "I dunno," in your sleep. You'll find yourself grinding your teeth when someone on the television says it.

"You don't know? He hit you for no reason at all?"

"Well…" Ahh, the unsure pause. Now we're getting somewhere.

"Well what?" You can also go with Letting the Uncomfortable Silence Stretch On. That works too.

"Well I pushed him but not that hard and then he hit me." The tattler never did anything to deserve it. At least, never anything that bad.

"You pushed him first?"

"Yeah, but not that hard. And then he hit me!"

"Why did you push him?"

Wait for it.

Wait…

"I dunno."

Then you need to find the hitter and go through the same process with that kid until you finally reach what feels like an approximation of the actual chain of events. I mean approximation. Sherlock Holmes would quit detecting after a day in a classroom. The mysteries are impossible and often impenetrable. Unless it was a big thing and seems like something that needs to go to the office, you should deal with it in-house with stern warnings and reflective questions about hitting and retaliation. These instances always peak at some point during the year, and that's when I bust out *The Butter Battle Book* by Dr. Seuss. Seuss, by the way, is the greatest author who ever lived. Yeah, that Bill Shakespeare guy was alright, but did he invent the Sneetches? I rest my case. Seuss also wrote a book for every single situation and they all have sneaky messages that are great fun to suss out with a class. Invest in Dr. Seuss books.

I know a teacher who created a Tattle Box one year because the tattling had gotten so bad in her room. The Tattle Box was a place where students could write down their tattle and place it in the box. She did not explain to the kids that at the end of every day, in front of them, she'd calmly go to the Tattle Box, take it to the garbage, and dump the contents without looking at a single paper. Now, this seems harsh, like she doesn't care what the kids are trying to tell her. The thing about a Tattle Box is the ones who use the box are filling it with reports on everyone else, and the ones still going to her had something serious to say. It's all about making expectations clear to your class, including what's an Important Report and what's a Tattle. You have to teach that. They don't know.

The best kind of tattling is when they tell on themselves. "Mr. Robertson, he's about to come over and tell you that I tripped him."

"Did you?"

"Uh." Gotcha. Thanks for making that so much easier.

Bodily Functions

Bodily functions will happen, there's no getting around it. Kids are gross. So much so in fact that my first book, *He's the*

Weird Teacher, has an entire chapter dedicated to how we deal with the icky that can be a child. The short version is- if a kid says he's going to be sick, don't question him. If a kid has to go to the bathroom *right now*, let him. Have boxes of tissues around the room. Have cleaner of some kind under the sink. Possibly a few kinds of cleaner. I know there's not a college class about what to do when you notice a puddle of pee in the concavity of a student's chair. The answer is to not make a big deal about it, you'll ruin the kid's day, week, month. Send the kid to the office to change. Dump the chair outside, hopefully you have access to an outside (but probably not out a second story window, though that might be funny in a sitcom kind of way). Get the custodian to wipe it down. Don't touch anything that comes out of anyone else's body. You stay cool, they'll stay cool. We're all cool in here Honey Bunny. Like the Fonz.

Crying

Tears happen. Even in the friendliest, happiest classes. Kids cry, it's ok. Sometimes they cry for what you would consider to be a good reason and sometimes you're wrong about it being a bad reason. No matter the reason, the big goal is to not make a kid feel worse than he or she already does. Take the student aside and try to get to the bottom of the tears without making a scene. Kids love to "help" their friend by forming a circle, making a ruckus, and asking loudly and repeatedly what's wrong. Will a student sometimes cry because being the center of attention like that is exactly the goal? Probably. Should we assume that going in? No. Help the student, give him or her a chance to collect themselves in the hallway or the bathroom. Sometimes it's because they think they did badly on an assignment. Sometimes kids cry and they don't know why. Sometimes they cry and they don't want to tell you why. Sometimes everyone else in the room will want to tell you why. There are too many variables for there to be one answer, except to be open and empathetic. You can't push a kid to tell you something they don't want to. You can make it clear with words and actions that you're there to listen.

Student teachers- lean on your mentor teachers for these things. Follow their lead, and trust your humanity. Reach for empathy first. But also know when you're out of your depth.

Occasionally, a student will have learned that tears can be weapons. There will have been an adult in their life who could be manipulated by tears, and they'll have learned that trouble goes away when the waterworks start. Again, don't assume this. But pay attention to the reasons behind the tears. Does the student feel terrible and that's making them cry? Are they watching you, waiting for you to soften because you feel badly? It's going to suck the first few times you make a student cry, because you will. Not on purpose, not because you're an awful person, but because you work with kids and sometimes it happens. It's also going to stop working on you. Probably once you watch a student turn the tears on and off like a Broadway player. Not every kid, not all the time, but you'll see this. Start from empathy.

"What's Racist?"

I was out of class for the day and a student asked my student teacher what racist was. She wasn't calling anyone racist, she wasn't being called racist, but it had come up at some point in her day and she wanted to know. My student teacher didn't know exactly how to handle it. It's a question with an obvious answer, but not necessarily an easy answer. There are many things teachers would try to keep in mind when answering such a pointed query. How conservative is the community? (Not judging conservative-leaning communities here, it's important to know your audience.) How can I answer this without it getting twisted around and ending up as parent phone calls? (Kids won't do this on purpose, mostly, but remember the game Telephone?) She wasn't sure how to juggle all of that, so she punted. She told the student that it's an excellent question and she would rather I answered it because she felt I could be clearer. She left unspoken than she wanted to hear how I answered it too.

These kinds of questions are what we call "teachable moments." All those concerns that I listed in the previous paragraph are legitimate, but I also think they aren't worth not being honest. I laid it out for the kid- it's hating someone for no good reason, hate because of the color of someone's skin, their religion, or some other superficial reason. It's a terrible thing. I went on to explain that sexist is a thing too, because as long as we're here we might as well go all in. This is an important topic. We were reading a wonderful book called *One Crazy Summer* by Rita Williams-Garcia that I couldn't recommend more for teachers fifth grade and up. It is great for these kinds of conversations. Student teachers- as a new teacher you might be hesitant to answer these kinds of questions like you want to. You're worried about parent phone calls and the like. I am not. I'll deal with whatever comes my way because education is about rooting out hate and ignorance with clarity and without fear. If I'm given the chance to do that, I'll take it every time. As a student teacher, maybe let your mentor teacher field that one. Learn how to fight the good fight in the smartest, most effective way.

Letter to Prison

That example from the beginning of this chapter was very

specific for a reason, it really happened to me my first year of teaching. And I really didn't know what to do. I told her to tell him how great she was doing in class and tell him about all the stuff she was learning and doing. That's the first but not the last time I've had a conversation with a kid about an incarcerated parent.

Then there's the other conversations school never prepared you for, like students getting kicked out of their homes, parents getting divorced (in my case personal experience helps with that so yay childhood pain coming back to be helpful), and other stories I can't even bring up because they're too specific and it's not my right or place. What I can say is you too will carry stories that you can tell, and stories you'll never share with anyone. Things you didn't want to know, but have to know to understand your kids. No matter how empathetic you think you are, there will be things during your student teaching year and every year thereafter that make you realize you know nothing.

You student teach so you can learn to use all the tools you were given in college.

You also student teach to start building the tools a college classroom can't possibly help you with because you have to experience it first.

Mentor teachers- preach empathy. Preach understanding. Don't shield your student teacher from these parts of the job, because these parts of the job are just as important as the pedagogy. Be open to the hard conversations. Open the hard conversations so your student teachers don't have to. Mentor honestly and with an open heart.

12. Difficult Conversations

But what if my student teacher isn't good at this?

This is a real concern for us, isn't it mentor teachers? What if the student I'm given doesn't seem to have the talent, patience, or indefinable *thing* that will make them a successful teacher? How do we have that conversation and what is there to do about it? I know there are some of you out there who have already answered this for yourself. "I tell them they are bad at this and maybe they should look at something else." That's an answer, but I'm not sure that's *the* answer.

We've established that everyone struggles in the classroom their first year. Their first two years. Maybe, probably, more. There's a difference between struggling and holy cow, what are you doing? Between "I wouldn't have taught that math lesson like that," and, "Oh, was that a math lesson? Huh." And I imagine that every mentor teacher's line of acceptable struggle is different. After all, these are our kids, our responsibility, and at some point we need to say, "Enough! No more."

But it should be rare that we try to chase someone out of the game all together. Except in rare cases, chasing someone away from teaching might constitute a failure on the part of the mentor teacher. What are some of the reasons for the difficult conversations we might have, and how should they be handled?

The Hateful

There are people who shouldn't be teachers, without question. The racist, sexist, bigoted. These people might sneak through the college system, though I don't know how. They must be good students. Not until they are actually in front of children do their fatal flaws appear. They have to be rooted out immediately. Education has no room for the hateful. It's our responsibility as mentor teachers to report them to the university and purge them from our ranks. The point of being a mentor teacher is to strengthen the profession. Letting people through who would disrespect our students and colleagues is doing a disservice to everyone.

The difficult conversation here would be, "What's your problem?" It's not actually that difficult of a conversation. Though you should be more tactful than that. Tact is a word I can spell, but not one I'm good at putting into practice. If I were given a student teacher who was sexist, racist, or homophobic, that person and I would have words almost immediately and wouldn't last. I would throw my weight around and do what I could to keep them out of the system. Don't argue that personal politics have no place in education, because I'm not talking politics here. I'm talking hate that makes the room unsafe. Disagreeing with your plan for the country's economy and disagreeing on whether or not gay people are ok are not the same thing and shouldn't be treated as such. You'll have gay students, and you need to be ok with that now. I want to be clear that I've never had this issue with a student teacher. I don't know anyone who has had this issue with a student teacher. But I do know there are hateful teachers in this country, and they must have gotten through the system somehow. As a peer to those people, I beg of them to leave, run, and never return. For the good of our profession. For the good of the students.

The Angry and Judgmental

The quick to anger and quick to judgement may also come

through our classrooms. Quick to anger is something I understand. It is something I've struggled with, though not to an extreme and not when it comes to students. But I get the college student who is angry and it's bubbling just below the surface, waiting for a reason to come out. The hard conversation here is about not just controlling the anger, that's not enough, but rooting out the source. Just like you would with an angry student. I would explain in simple, clear terms that anger has no place in a classroom. It's not a useful emotion often in life in general, and it's even less useful with children. Some of our kids get the anger at home so much that you're just going to be one more vein-popped red-face in their lives, and one more of those is the last thing the kid needs. They're desensitized to it anyway, you're wasting your breath. Or you're going to scare the kids into submission and, great, now they won't do anything and you've created a classroom with almost as much joy as a Borg Cube. Find a way past that, and find the joy in education.

Quick to judgement sounds a lot like racist/sexist/homophobic student teachers, but with one key difference- they're willing to learn. The judgement comes from a place of ignorance rather than hate. I'm splitting hairs, but this is important. Students who say, "Those kids," without the vitriol. These are people we can reach. These conversations are hard because confronting someone about their biases is never easy. As humans, we naturally push back against that type of confrontation. Anyone who has sat in a meeting where a presenter is talking about race and says something along the lines of, "You are treating your black students differently than your white students," and has felt the staff recoil as if it say, "How *dare* you suggest I'm racist," knows this feeling. Those who need this conversation are student teachers who come to us with biases so ingrained they don't know they're there. Often the difficult conversations are actually a series of smaller teachable moments, correcting of lessons plans, and constructive feedback that leads to the student teacher finding the greater understanding themselves. There's only so much a mentor teacher can do before the student teacher has to find their own way. There is room for big, long, honest conversations in this. The trick for us, mentor teachers, is not to accuse. Accusations put shields up. Ask guiding questions that force self-reflection. Give examples. But we cannot let it pass uncommented upon. A student teacher who is quick to judge with their mentor teacher in the room with them will only get quicker and more judgmental without interference and in their own classrooms.

The above are extreme cases. And, I believe, rare cases. Except that last one, the judgmental one. I think there's more people in education (student teachers and otherwise) that fall into that category than would ever admit it. We must listen to others and confront the biases within ourselves.

Setting Expectations And Why So Lazy

There are a lot of definitions of lazy depending on who you are and what your own personal work ethic is. There are as many schools of thought on how much time a teacher should spend in their classroom and at home working and preparing as there are schools in the world. Lazy is something a mentor teacher needs to define for themselves, and then define clearly for their student teacher. The key to avoiding this conversation completely is to frame it in a positive way (this is always a good way to approach hard topics). Don't start with, "I don't like it when student teachers blah blah blah." Start with, "I love it when student teachers blah blah blah." Classroom rules should be written the same. Avoid negatives, promote positives. Make your expectations for your student teacher's work ethic crystal clear from the jump. It's part of my early conversations.

"School starts at this time. I will be here at this time, and so will you so that we can talk over the day and make sure any last minute issues are resolved. We're going to chat after school every day, so make sure you're good with that. I love it when student teachers ask me to teach lessons, even if you don't know what exactly you want to teach. You can ask me to see the standards, but I will look the same place you will- the magical land of The Interwebs. If you come to me and say, 'I was looking at the standards and have an idea for a science lesson that fits this,' I'll buy you a coffee."

Make expectations clear and positive. The only negatively-tinged thing I say in those early conversations is, "If you don't respect our kids there will be a problem." That's all I need to say, and often I can even preface that statement with, "I know I don't need to tell you this, but I'm going to anyway to be sure I said it." Saying things out loud that you might think are best left unsaid will help avoid confusion later.

If I do notice that a student teacher isn't pulling their weight I'm not going to be shy about it. Shy, like tact, is a word I'm aware of but have never internalized to any useful degree. This, by the way, is something I need to be aware of when creating presentation projects, because I always forget about my introvert kids and need to go back and rejigger things to be friendly for all. This also goes for student teachers struggling with specific subjects or topics. Don't wait, have the conversation, figure out what's wrong, and take action. Or send them to a teacher who is better at it than you. There's not enough time in a school year to be shy about correcting issues with a student teachers. In the words of Willy Wonka, "There's so much time and so little to do. Wait a minute. Strike that. Reverse it."

Often a difficult conversation about a lazy student teacher isn't called for at all. Not if the relationship has been set up and strengthened over time. Not if you both have a baseline of honesty and a shared goal of Better For The Kids. Then every corrective conversation is supported with understanding. Then you get around hard conversations before they get difficult. If you do reach a place where the difficult conversation is needed, explain where you're coming from and specifically what you're seeing that reads as lazy. Let the student teacher explain. Try to avoid accusations. Do this during your meeting times. That's what they're for.

Ego

Student teachers- do not be afraid to ask for critiques. Your ego is less important than student learning. Mentor teachers- our ego is less important than student or student teacher learning. We must all be open to the idea that ego is a barrier to learning, and that it exists in a very real way.

There is no room for ego in the student teacher/mentor teacher relationship. Mentor teachers- the title Mentor comes with ego if we're not careful. "You should listen to me. I am your MENTOR, after all." Tack onto that the built-in power dynamic of the relationship and add the comparative experience levels and it becomes exceptionally easy to pack your bags and take that power trip without even knowing it. Mentor teachers keeping our heads in the game and constantly reflecting on the Why Did I Do/Say That aspects of mentoring will help. Ego will prevent us from being the best mentor teacher we can be because it will blind us to good ideas that we didn't come up with. Too much ego means we won't hear anyone else.

Now, simply by volunteering to be a mentor teacher we are showing some level of ego. Along with saying, "Yes, I am able to train a future teacher," we should also say, "Though my ego is not so big that I think I know everything." (Now imagine that you're a mentor teacher *and* you decide to write a book for other mentor teachers and student teachers. Can you imagine the ego on that guy? Oy.)

Student teachers- ego is a protective shell, not a protective barrier. Barrier suggests strength. It's a shell. It's fragile and easily cracked and inside there's a baby teacher unsure if he or she is ready for the world. Your ego might come up after a bad lesson. "Those kids just did not want to learn today. Why weren't they paying attention?" You see where the ego in those sentences is? It's where you're blaming the kids instead of reflecting on your own performance. It saves your delicate skin from the burn of a badly taught lesson. Let those thoughts happen, but then see them for what they are and go back and look again, deeper.

Ego isn't always a bad thing. **The only thing to be hardline about is not being hardline about anything**. Ego can force you to be better if you have a healthy grasp on it. I constantly use my ego to come up with a better lesson. Yes, always for the kids, but also because I know I wasn't good enough last time. I could be more on point, give a better lesson, hit those standards harder, give the kids more freedom, find more creative ways to do something. All of those are ego triggers for me. As long as I don't get caught up in them, it's all good. One of my favorite jokes, and I say this to my class and to my student teachers, is, "It's not a competition, but we're going to win."

"When we go to the assembly we're going to be the best class in there. It's not a competition, but we're going to win."

"When you go back to your student teaching cohort and talk about the awesome things we did in class this week they're going to be so impressed. It's not a contest, of course, but you're still going to win."

Education shouldn't be a contest. It can be, and if you look at graduation rates compared to suspension rates you'll see that the system is often designed to create winners and losers. But it shouldn't be. "We're going to win," is a joke. A joke with a taste of the truth, which the best jokes have. I do want my class to be the best in the school. I do want every other teacher to look to my kids and think, "Wow, that class is on it and they are doing awesome work." As a mentor teacher, I do want my student teacher to be learning more, be teaching more, and be getting the best care. I want other student teachers to be just a little bit jealous, and I want other mentor teachers to use that to make themselves better. It's not a contest because if all of us get better together then all of us win, guiding better and better classes of student teachers into their own classes. It's not a real contest because if it were why write books sharing what I think are the best techniques and ideas? I'd keep all that to myself. Then I'd win but the profession would lose out. (Woo, dig that sentence, speaking of ego, huh?) We should all be sharing and cooperating.

Difficult conversations are important to have. They breed honesty, and the student teacher/mentor teacher relationship needs honesty to be effective. To grow stronger and better together.

13. Teacher Senses

Student teachers- I know who you are. I know what you want. If you're looking for great pay, I can tell you you won't have a ton of money. But what I do have, and you will learn, are a very particular set of senses. Senses I have acquired over a very long career. Senses that mean I can help you develop your own set of Teacher Senses so you too can paraphrase the famous TAKEN speech out of context whenever you want to confuse your students and amuse yourself.

These are those senses.

Teacher Voice

Teachers don't yell. It doesn't work. You can't possibly be louder than a classroom full of students for any length of time. You'll want to yell. It won't do any good. Don't yell. Your Teacher Voice Swiss Army knife won't have a yell option that's worth a damn.

Teachers are on stage. Even those who subscribe the the philosophy that lecture is terrible have to agree that sometimes you need to be heard by the whole room. Your Teacher Voice is not dissimilar to an actor's voice. We project, from the front of the room to the back, without shouting. It comes from the diaphragm and is pushed through your belly, not your throat. No matter what, your throat will hurt the first week of school. You've never talked this much, this firmly, in your life, unless you are an actor-type. Projecting through your diaphragm will prevent you from going completely hoarse and will help you control your tone and volume. Back straight, shoulders back, chin up, let the airway stay open so your voice flows smoothly and without interruption. Projecting does not mean you're stuck in one tone of voice, and it's not barking like a drill sergeant. All you're doing is helping your voice carry to all ears in the room. This is yet another reason that, if I designed Teacher Prep programs, I'd include Acting 101 as a required course.

Your instinct when speaking to a loudly working room of students (noise doesn't equal off task, remember that. Given the correct assignment, noise can mean great learning is happening) is to speak over the room. Resist this urge. Do not train your kids to listen for you speaking over them. If they are actually having valuable conversations, or are in the midst of off-task conversations that are more interesting than you, you being louder than them results in one thing: Them being louder than you. This becomes a tug-of-war you will lose.

You need to find a way to get the volume down before you start talking. Teachers have many tricks for this. Call and response is popular- Class class/Yes yes. Ba-dada-ba-ba/Ba-ba. I use counting down because it's easy to remember and provides some flexibility depending on if I'm counting from five or three. A personal favorite is also, "Raise your hand if you can hear me." This is said at a lower-than-normal volume so that the kids nearest to you hear you and stop, and then you repeat yourself until the room is quiet and everyone is looking at you with their hand up except for one kid who is still talking away to his partner completely oblivious to the looks he's getting. This isn't a routine that immediately quiets the class, but also doesn't take as long as you might think, especially once they've been through it once or twice. Please don't use a whistle. I'm not big on bells either, though I use a timer so I'm also a hypocrite. A timer going off seems different than ringing a bell at my kids like I'm Mr. Pavlov.

Volume modification, by the way, is a valuable tool. Dynamics work because they sound off and therefore get attention. But don't go louder, always go quieter. I'm constantly amazed by teachers with the softest, quietest voices who hold their classes in the palms of their hands. But what else are the kids to do? If you're quiet and they want to hear you, they have to be quiet too. This is a trick that I know, and I use when I think of it, but I'm naturally loud so it's a conscious effort for me to bring it down.

One voice that you'll have to develop is your true Teacher Voice, known between student teachers and myself as the, excuse the adult language, No Bullshit Voice. The only other time you'll have used a NBV is if you were a lifeguard. It's voice that conveys a lot of information in very few words. There's a command tone in it. When I do it, my voice deepens. Humans know how to hear the NBV, and can read it fairly well. It's not something you come by naturally because the line between the NBV and sounding angry can be thin. It's stern, and comes with a Teacher Look, which I'll get to.

The most important part of your Teacher Voice is remembering that you're communicating more than words (to show how you feel). You're communicating emotion. The main emotion of your classroom should be joy. Speak with a smile, even when you're not feeling it. People can hear a smile. Your students will respond better to a smile than to a scowl. At the very least, don't let anger creep into your voice. Kids don't need your anger. Think about your parents. "I'm just...disappointed," works better anyway.

Listen to your mentor teacher's many voices and note how

the kids respond. Literally, make note of it in your journal. Then talk about it afterwards. Ask why your mentor teacher said what they said how they said it. Mentor teachers- we should be prepared to answer these questions or prepared to reflect on why we can't. Having someone hear how we talk to our kids will help us better modulate our tones and reflect on why we speak how we do.

Teacher Ears

Prepare to hear better than you've ever heard before. Prepare for students to be amazed at how well you hear because they don't realize that whisper-shouting is still shouting. Prepare to pretend you heard more than you did to get a kid to tell you what she said.

You will soon become attuned to certain tones of voice. The way a child's voice changes when he leans over to tell his friend a joke. You'll be able to tell the difference between a snicker and a giggle and a chuckle. Eventually. To start it will all be too much information to process. You won't even know what you're missing because you'll be too busy trying to hear everything and remember what you're supposed to be doing and following your internal flow chart of If a Student Does This Then I Do That. Don't worry, it'll come.

This is a Small Rock your mentor teacher should work on with you once they think you're ready. Make it a lesson goal for a bit, to find out what you hear on the periphery. When you're able to pay attention to more things at once, pay attention to the purposefully quiet noises in the room. There's a lot of information there.

Student teachers who are parents or who have experience with small people- you have an advantage in Teacher Hearing because Parent Hearing operates in much the same way. You know what movies mean when an actor says, "It's quiet. Too quiet." Parent Voice and Teacher Voice have a lot of crossover too, which is why I get annoyed at home when one of my children makes me use my Teacher Voice.

Parents have another skill non-parents will have to learn-you're able to decode a child's specific dialect. Some kids speak in such a way that unless you know the kid you won't have any idea what they're saying. It's similar to understanding heavily accented English. You need to learn to listen more carefully. You will have students who you understand perfectly well that other adults won't understand at all, and you'll get to translate (See also Eyes, Teacher). Unfortunately, there will still be students who speak so quietly that you'll never hear them clearly until you help them learn to speak up.

My favorite Teacher Ears story comes from a third grade class I taught in Hawaii. I tell this story in *He's the Weird Teacher* but it bears repeating here. I was walking my room while students were quietly working on something when I heard one student lean over to another and whisper, "Suck it!" These are good kids. I was sure I'd misheard. That's not possibly what was whispered. Then he did it again, more insistently. "Suck it!"

I swiftly moved to intercept and leaned down between the two, "What did you say?"

The student looked innocently up at me and replied, "I told him to suck it."

"Wh-What? Why? What?"

He looked even more innocent, "It'll feel better if he sucks it." I had no response except to carefully repeat my previous question. He looked at me like I was dense, held up his hand, and said, "He's got a papercut. It'll feel better if he sucks it."

Teacher Eyes

Argus of Greek mythology was a giant with a hundred eyes. You will be like Argus. You will learn to see everything. There should be conversations early in the year between student teacher and mentor teacher where the mentor teacher asks if the student teacher noticed something in the back of the room and the student teacher has no idea what the mentor teacher is talking about. Those conversations later in the year come in the form of the student teacher telling the mentor teacher what she saw before the mentor teacher brings it up.

Like Teacher Ears, much of this comes with practice and confidence. It's yet another reason mentor teachers **need to have student teachers in front of the class as often as possible**. The only way to develop these senses is to teach and teach and teach. All of them are Small Rocks. You can only focus on all the things you should be seeing after you've gotten past the stage of trying to remember all the lesson plan steps and basic discipline tricks.

Teacher Eyes allow you to see who's working, who's pretending to work, and who is uninterested in maintaining the façade any longer. The line between the first two is the one you'll need to learn to walk. On top of that, and this comes with time, experience, and even then you still won't be great at it, Thinking and Spacing Out look exactly the same. Is that student over there on Mars, or is he planning out what he's going to write next? The only way to know is to ask. I will repeat this over and over and over, assume the best.

Teacher Eyes come with the Teacher Look. The Teacher Look has been known to freeze a troublemaker in his tracks at 100 yards. The Teacher Look is a form of mind control, as it alone can help a student choose between the best choice and the not-so-much choice. The Teacher Look can be felt through the back of the head. At first your Teacher Look might be more like Crazy Eyes McGee, but eventually you'll learn the slight hardening of the gaze, the infinitesimal tensing of the muscles around the eyes, the slight angle of the eyebrows. With a Look you'll be able to say, "I see you about to pass that note, and I don't want to make a big deal out of it. There's nothing in there that can't wait until recess. Please put it away and get back to work. Thank you." Students will learn to read your Teacher Looks, especially if you're explicit with them at first and do the narration out loud. Students have Looks too, by the way. Enjoy decoding those.

Teacher Eyes also work like Teacher Ears in that you and you alone will be able to read the handwriting of your students. "But Doug," you protest. "My kids will all be typing, so handwriting won't be a issue." Ha, yes it will. They'll still write some things. There's no reason to go completely paperless. Remember, balance in all things. Besides, spell check won't know what the heck they're trying to type some of the time. You will be able to decode their spelling and make sense of the sentence with no vowels. You'll help them rewrite their work so the rest of the world can see their brilliance as well as you can.

Teacher Presence

Confidence stands differently than unsurety. Your Teacher Presence sends a message to your class. Are you slouched and slow-moving, tired? They won't know if you're tired from a long night or tired of them. Are you bristling and covered with thorns, because they can see that too and read that it means Stay Away. Are you mad at them or at something else? Kids tend to center themselves in the universe, so they'll assume your emotional state is related to them. This is important to remember, so I'm going to write it again. *Kids tend to center themselves in the universe, so they'll assume your emotional state is related to them.* Regardless of whether it is or not. Know what your body language says, it's a language everyone speaks, but not everyone speaks fluently. Best to stand relaxed but confident, sure of yourself and in control, even if you're neither. The least-stressed looking person on any team should be the leader, because that attitude is caught by the rest of the team. You're team leader.

Teacher Presence is kind of indefinable. Many of the best teachers I've been around feel completely present and at ease in the room. They have a sense of ownership about them. It looks different on everyone. But students know it. When you move through the room your aura moves with you. Teacher Presence is the reason proximity works as a behavior modifier. It's not that you should loom over a student, but sometimes sitting right on that shoulder for a second is all you need to do to get someone back on task.

Your Teacher Presence should make students feel comfortable and at ease. When you speak to a child who is sitting or shorter than you, go down to their level. No one likes looking up at someone, and mitigating the built-in power differential will make your classroom a happier place.

Watch your mentor teacher for how they move around the room, how they stand and sit, and where and when. Look at their body language and ask them to look at yours. Recording yourself teaching is no one's idea of a good time, but along with using it to find all the little tics you didn't know you had, you'll also be able to see what your body is communicating to your students and increase your awareness.

Teacher Time

"Hasn't she been in the bathroom a long time?" you'll say. You didn't look at the clock. You don't have a timer running. What you do have is an internal clock that will be getting more precise by the day. By the lesson. Which is why **mentor teachers should be having student teachers teach as much as possible**.

I use a timer for everything. It keeps me on track. I keep an eye on my classroom clock. But I'm also fairly confident that if I was asked to teach an hour long lesson without using a clock I could land within five minutes on either side. This is an old runner trick I used to use. If you go on vacation in the midst of training, go for a three mile or half hour long (you pick the time or distance) run without looking at your watch or GPS monitor. Run by feel. When you get back to your starting point, check how you did. It's instructive to see if your body has learned what a specific time and distance feels like. Making lessons fit between snack and lunch works in much the same way.

You and your mentor teacher will spend plenty of time pacing out lessons. You are going to think things will take longer than they actually do. Accept this now. Better to over-plan. I got it real bad when I was a student teacher. I spent eight weeks in a GATE (Gifted And Talented Education) classroom. These were the kids who tested as the highest of high-fliers, and they were all put into one room. We're not going to go into how I feel about that now, after a few years teaching (Short answer: Ugh. Ick. Ew. No). What I will say is those kids worked at warp speed, and I consistently shorted my lessons. As in, I'd hand something out and by the time the last kid got the work the first kid would be done. I should note that I had a much less helpful mentor teacher in that placement than in my second grade placement.

Timing comes with time. Plan carefully, and trust your mentor teacher when they tell you that you are under- or over-estimating how long something is going to take.

Mentor teachers- let your student teacher go too short and too long a few times once you think they're ready. It's good practice for a student teacher to have to find ways to fill time effectively or end a lesson prematurely without bringing everything to a crashing halt.

Teacher Brain

Your teacher brain is what brings all of these elements together in harmony. As you strengthen one element, so shall you strengthen the others.

Your Teacher Brain is also what will jump up in the middle of a vacation and say, "Wait, we're on the Big Island of Hawaii! We need to go to Volcano National Park and take a bunch of pictures. I bet they have books there too. And a map I could put up in my room. And postcards I could give my kids. Why are you still on the beach, let's go!" It's never going to go away, so instead of trying to quiet it, encourage it. When you get a bit of inspiration, write it down somewhere. When you're shopping at a fabric store, your Teacher Brain will think, "I bet I can figure out something to do with that discounted felt over there." That means it's time to make some puppets. Why? You'll figure out a reason. Puppets are cool and kids love them.

Your Teacher Brain will annoy your non-teacher friends. Especially if you teach little kids. You will find your friends looking at you impatiently and you'll realize that you were just explaining something to them as though they were five. Whoops.

They don't need that. Except your buddy Matt. He totally does.

Teacher Nose

You'll be more sensitive to smells. That's...that's all I'm going to say.

14. Dear Universities

To my friends and colleagues at the university level,

I want to preface everything I'm about to say by admitting that, as a teacher, it's hard to hear someone who doesn't do my job tell me how I could do my job better. However, the closer that person is to my actual job, the easier it is to hear. You understand, you do this job too. Your in-law's best friend, the bartender, the dude next to you on the airplane, they all have opinions about education, and might even have some good ideas, but they don't land with the force of your principal's or of a peer two classrooms over whose work you respect and admire. I feel that, as a multi-time, multi-state mentor teacher, I have learned something of how teacher prep programs work. Not in the in-law's best friend's, "I was also in school once so I know things," way, but in the, "I have a direct connection to what you do," way. I've spent a lot of time working with student teachers and helping them navigate the twin challenges of learning to teach while remaining a good student. This is also the point where I acknowledge that there are as many teacher preparation courses as there are stars in the sky, and not all of what I'm about to say will apply to all of them. So it goes. I honestly believe you are doing your best to prepare your students to be teachers. I also honestly believe that you, like all of us, could be doing this better.

All that to say, I have thoughts. (You should see my principal's expression when she hears me utter those words.)

Tech? Tech.

Where's the edtech training? What kind of technology

integration is happening at the university level and why isn't it as evident as it ought to be in the student teachers coming to us from your programs? Every single Methods-level course should be demanding students organically integrate technology into most of their lessons. All forms of technology. And in a wide variety of technological-level settings, from 1:1 to wind-up desktop. Students making another slideshow does not count.

Is time being taken to not only teach what flipped and blended lessons are, but to model them and have students practice creating them? The first time a student makes a video lesson should not be in their mentor teacher's room. The amount of time saved on the part of the mentor teacher would be immense if we didn't have to teach that skill. Plus, this is a place where the student could become the master and teach their mentor teacher. Video editing, quick one-shot videos, sharing videos, these should be skills built in at all levels. Much like I can't assume my students know how to use computers, don't forget that digital natives don't exist, your programs should not assume that your students will know how to teach with technology.

Student teachers should be coming to us with facility in all operating systems. They should have a background in basic coding. They should have seen and worked with simple robots. They should be filled to the brim with the latest edtech know-how, because that stuff moves remarkably fast and this will give them the leg-up they need to keep up without sprinting right off the mark.

Go beyond document sharing and word processing. Get deep. Find educational technology conferences and send your kids. (As an aside, edtech conferences should grant *massive* discounts to student teachers. On the order of 75-80% off the sticker price. Or should be completely free. Why? Because, like the song says, "I believe the children are our future." Tech Conferences- you're making bank on the vendors, I've seen those halls. Hook student teachers up.) Done correctly this will not interfere with what you're already doing in class. That's why the word is *integrate* and not *replace*. I want a student teacher who knows what to do if she comes to my room and I've got 1:1 tablets, 1:1 laptops, or two giant, ancient desktops. I want a student teacher who believes BYOD (Bring Your Own Device) is a viable and useful option and knows how to guide students to responsible choices within a BYOD program.

I want a student teacher unafraid to find a new program, pull it up, and push buttons until it does something vaguely educational. I want a student teacher so well-versed in technology that she can look at any lesson plan and start to find ways to add value through a variety of technologies.

I can teach this once they're in my classroom, and I will. But if you're preparing them to enter the workforce, prepare them to enter above and beyond what the people who are already there can do. New teachers need every advantage we can give them. It is hard enough learning a new curriculum. Learning to integrate technology at the same time is a big ask. Let's work together to make sure they hit the ground well-prepared.

Student teachers- I'll say it again: Being good with educational technology will get your hired. That's not the biggest reason you should get good at it, but it sure is a nice carrot.

Movement

Schools are moving beyond park-and-bark teaching, and have been for a while. University programs should be preparing student teachers to integrate movement into their lessons. Cover things like alternative seating choices. Help student teachers learn that kids should not be stuck at their desks all day, there are better ways to learn. Help mentor teachers know this is coming as well. Much like technology integration, movement should not be a separate lesson. This is holistic lesson planning. Get student teachers moving in their classes so they know how to get students moving. Get them over being shy or feeling silly before they get to us.

Student teachers should be doing research projects on the value of movement-based learning and what types of movement promote what types of energy. I want to be planning a lesson alongside my student teacher and have him point at the lesson plan and say, "You know what we could do? Right here, let's change this to Four Corners or Charades. We have all this whiteboard space, why aren't the students doing the work up here?" And I want those ideas to be planted in their university courses. I want it to be on the rubrics by which their lessons are graded.

Project-Based Learning and Alternative Assessments

Spend time on Project-Based learning. I hope that university students are moving away from learning how to write the best test, or find the best test in the book or online, and are moving towards finding the best assessment. The goal is to see how well students are learning something, and often a paper-pencil test isn't the tool that will do that job. Students should be making things, creating projects. A test is a form of assessment, but it's not the only form. Please be sure to be keeping their scope wide open.

Keep this in mind as you teach your students- a good project is one that results in as many different final products as there are students in the class, and one that allows a student the freedom to demonstrate their learning in a variety of ways. Are students able to make a video, build a thing, draw a comic, or give a speech to present their project? They should be. This should be modelled in Methods classes. Lip-service teaches no one anything. If you tell your student teachers they should be having their classes use project-based learning, then in your Methods classes you should be allowing projects as assessments.

I know student teachers are training in the ancient and sacred art of rubric making, and that's good. Keep that up, but make sure not to make the rubrics overly complicated. A child should be able to read it, because a child is the one who will be using it. Percentages and averages don't tell the story. Please don't teach a student teacher to average grades, that's not a measure of what a kid knows now. It's not tracking growth and current learning. Let's say I bomb an early math test, but I study and work hard and my math grades slowly improve until I get a 98% on the final test of the section. When you are calculating grades for that section, why would you punish me for a terrible score from a month ago when I've clearly learned the material since? The student's goal isn't numbers-based, it's learning-based. Student teachers- grading is something you'll do because it's part of teaching. We give grades, we give report cards, it's the system. Grades rarely reflect learning accurately, but the best kind of grades are standards-based and reflect current growth. Students need lots of feedback, just like you do.

Any project that ends with a student wanting to do another project, or go back and make that project better, was a good project.

Lesson Planning

Ok, I know why student teachers have to write the giant, five-page, hyper-detailed lesson plans. I do. It's Big Rocks. It's covering all the bases and being sure that the student teacher knows what they're saying, why they're saying it, who they're saying it to, for how long it'll all be said, and what happens after all is said and done. I agree. It's important. I tell my student teachers as much.

I still think there's a line where enough is enough, and many programs refuse to cross this line in favor of being really really really really really sure the student teacher is ready. I can hear the student teachers reading this getting their highlighters out, ready to mark this section up and present it triumphantly to their university coordinators and professors. Cap those pens, my friends. More is still better. The Big Rocks matter, and they're heavier than you think. More assures that you know what you're doing.

But because I also believe we should never be hardline about anything in education, and I believe our expectations should reflect individual learners, can we also start teaching our student teachers how to pare down these lessons into something that will more closely resemble what they'll be doing in their own classrooms? The entire goal of all of this, say it with me, is to be sure each and every student in the program is able to get a job, walk confidently into that job on their first day, and continue to successfully do that job through those early weeks and months. Let lesson planning become flexible as the year progresses. After a certain date allow *x* number of submitted lesson plans to fit a more abbreviated format. This would be a perfect chance for the university coordinator and the mentor teacher to work together with the student teacher to develop a more individualized plan. If the student teacher is having an overall successful year and showing growth, official lesson plans can become simpler. If not, the format remains the longer-form, more detailed outlines. Student teachers would still need to know the learning goals, the steps they will be taking to ensure the learning goals are being achieved, and the things they are doing during the lesson. But they'll save time for themselves in the writing of it all, time which could be spent getting creative with the lesson instead, finding ways to add technology or movement or art, time that could be spent finding more student choice and voice options. Great lesson plans are like Lego bricks. You should be able to add and subtract pieces based on what you're building and who is doing the building. Because once the student teachers have their own classrooms they'll never write a giant lesson plan like that again.

To be frank, when my student teacher and I plan the non-program required lessons they'll teach, we don't get too detailed in the writing unless we need to. This is after, of course, I feel the student teacher has moved past the need to write down every single, "I Say then Students Say." Between you and me, we both know those hyper-detailed lesson plans never shake out like they're written anyway. Man plans, a room full of fifth graders laughs. Making student teachers constantly write highly detailed lesson plans long after they need to is all part of the eternal educational struggle to quantify something that isn't clearly quantifiable.

Speaking of that…

Evaluations

I signed up for this. I understood the sacrifices I'd be making. I knew that multiples times during the school year I'd be sitting at my desk with a long bubble sheet of evaluation questions and criteria and going over it with my student teacher.

I get it. You need the data. You need evidence for grades and certifications and to cover your tails in case a student teacher's experience goes badly. I'm pretty sure I'm tilting at windmills here.

So rather than ask you to do away with mentor teacher evaluations completely, which is silly (never be hardline blah blah blah), how about working with mentor teachers to design the best, most streamlined version of an evaluation? An example- I recently filled out an evaluation with the question, "Teacher candidate demonstrates a tolerance for ambiguity." This came with a 1-4 rating choice. Every single time I came to this question I wanted to skip the numbers and write, "Meh." It struck me as funny that I needed to put a specific number to ambiguity. In my room in particular, ambiguity is the name of the game. Ambiguity gives flexibility and freedom. Student teachers should be great at ambiguity. But in other rooms, with other mentor teachers, this is not the case. Other teachers hate ambiguity. We can do better with these evaluations. Yes, what I'm suggesting will create more work, but it will also yield better, more actionable results.

If mentor teachers are following my advice and meeting daily with their student teachers then these evaluations are the easiest things in the world. Like a student's report card, there will be no surprises when it comes time to do the paperwork because the student teacher has been in on the learning every step of the way.

Again, I know you have to do these things. I know why they have to be done. I get it. They're like report cards, part of the system. I'm still going to complain about the extra paperwork. Speaking of- it really shouldn't be paperwork, it should be digital.

Don't hand me a packet. Email me a link.

Official and Drop-In Observations

Student teachers get stressed out when their university coordinator is coming to observe them. Which makes sense, the coordinator's opinion holds sway over their future. Hopefully they aren't stressed because they want a good grade. Grades aren't a good motivator with students. But what exactly is being looked for in these observations? I have this same question when it comes to my own principal's observations, and have for years. What, specifically, is being looked for? Yes, you have a rubric, but are you focusing on the right things?

See, I think most observations are looking at *Teaching* when they should be looking at *Learning*. Are you coming in to see how well a student teacher Teaches, or how well the student teacher's class is Learning what's being taught? These are two different things. Teaching is performative. I call it "Capital-T Teaching". We know what Teaching looks like. We've seen it in movies and professional development videos with preternaturally well-behaved students in tiny classes. We also know all the little engagement tricks teachers have to keep kids focused and on task. I'm not taking away from these engagement tricks, they're great. They're especially great when someone is watching you Teach. There's a million videos online of Great Teachers Teaching. But almost all of those are also Great Teachers Talking. Great Teachers Asking Questions And Students Responding.

If we're looking for Learning, that's something completely different. When I'm observed I love to mess with the system by planning a student-centered lesson that has me doing almost no Teaching. And I'm great at Teaching. I'm engaging and funny and the kids, for the most part, love being part of the show. Observe me Teach and you'll see me doing some great work.

It's more fun, and more effective, if I'm focused on the students' Learning. I shouldn't be the one doing the work. I encourage student teachers to do observation lessons where we tell the kids, "Were doing Tableaux. Here's a quick reminder of what it is (Tableaux is a vocabulary game where the kids have to define words by creating shapes with their bodies and not moving. Think charades, but holding still.). Choose three vocabulary words. Don't forget to use your high, medium, and low levels, and face your audience. Find groups aaaaaaand go." That's the extent of the Teaching. Now the student teacher mixes through the room, working with groups, encouraging creativity, checking for understanding, clarifying. Then the class makes a circle and each group runs through their Tableaux. The student teacher guides on the side and leads the class in giving feedback to their peers. This is a much more effective vocabulary lesson than a traditionally Taught lesson might be. It's got movement and student choice and voice and there's laughing and freedom. But there's very little Teaching, and as a result student teachers are hesitant to use it and lessons like it for their observations.

That's a problem. They should know that you're coming in to see how well they facilitate learning amongst their students, not how well they perform. University supervisors, for the most part, love these Learning lessons. But, it does not feel like student teachers are ever told they want to see these kinds of Learning lessons. Student teachers think their coordinators want to see Teaching. Let's move past that and make it clear you're looking for Learning.

Preparing Mentor Teachers

Part of the reason this book exists is because I don't feel mentor teachers are as prepared to be mentor teachers as student teachers need them to be. I think universities should be better at making expectations clear, and giving guidance about what makes a great mentor teacher. I think it should be more than an email or a packet. It should be an hour or two at least, a class we're paid to go to. Do not assume that because a teacher is good with second graders that he will be good with a college student. Mentor teaching and teaching small children are the same skillset, but used differently and with different aims. Time should be taken to be sure mentor teachers know what they're getting into and what their student teachers will need.

If giving them this book happens to be part of that process, well, so be it.

The End of the Year

Everything comes to a head at the end of the school year, and it's not fair to anyone. Student teachers often have their Big Papers At The End to do. They are also supposed to be soloing, or whatever form of soloing their particular program encourages. The end of the year in the student teacher's placement is also the time of The Big Test At The End and all the end of year paperwork and report cards and so on and so forth. The end of the school year is crazy, and I don't think universities pace their programs to take all of this into account. The current teaching certificate Big Thing is called the edTPA, and it's a massive undertaking that calls for multiple lessons to be taught and recorded, thousands of words to be written, and dozens of hoops to be jumped through. Far be it from me to say the way this is put together is wrong, though it seems like an awful lot from where I'm sitting. I'm sure the intention is good and many meetings took place. Lots of boxes to check, many "t"s to dot and "i"s to cross. There shall be Accountability and it shall be Rigorous!

I kid. I know that creating a statewide system to try and guarantee a teacher is ready is nearly impossible. I also know that what does currently exist does not capture the true ability of a student teacher. Such is the struggle with a broad spectrum requirement system.

So instead what I'm asking is that universities think before they make things due. Work with mentor teachers and their administrators, talk to student teachers, and find ways for everyone to be successful without burning out. Burnout is a very real problem in education, and student teachers should know that teaching is hard, but not that it's an exhausting profession that will consume your every waking minute for months on end. That's not healthy or helpful. In the long run, it's probably damaging. We must walk the line between making it hard and realistic and running our kids so ragged they sleep for a week after the year ends and question their life choices. This isn't the Marines in some movie. A healthy teacher is a happy teacher, and a happy teacher is a better teacher.

One of the major goals of mentor teachers, student teachers, and university programs should be striving to make all aspects of teacher preparation better. It'll never be a perfect system. Education isn't perfect. It's a living thing that must grow and evolve and adapt constantly. Together we should be willing to do that.

15. Watch Me Rebuild

The student teacher who wrote the foreword for this book was with me during one of the most challenging years of my teaching career. Without her it would have been even more trying. She learned a lot that year. So did I.

It was a fifth grade class with 36 students in it. Some of you just read that number three times and experienced a sharp tightness in your chest. Or you scoffed and thought about the year you had forty kids. Or you're an upper grade teacher and you scoffed because you have, all told, over a hundred kids. My only counter to that is yeah, but not all at once, and you don't have to do every single subject for all of those kids. I'm not minimizing the struggle. Every classroom every year has unique challenges and we should recognize that. This was my situation and class size.

Student teachers- thirty-six might not mean much to you yet because you don't have any context for what that looks like when you're expected to be teaching all of them. You should know that it's a lot of kids. No matter how good at this you are, that's a lot of bodies in one room, and it's a lot of minds to be responsible for.

Among those 36 were many with IEPs, some without IEPs at the start who started the placement process with us, a handful of second language learners, and a couple of kids that struggle with their choices, making everything more of a challenge. Not because they were bad kids, but because their needs and personalities seem to take up more of the room. Classrooms are like laboratories, and students are chemicals. When you are doing chemistry you learn that when you combine these two chemicals you get a flash of light, while if you combine those two you get a puff of smoke. So you try combining the flash of light chemical combination with one of the puff of smoke chemicals and you end up with an explosion. My student teacher and I had a lot of chemicals that needed specific bonding choices. Not a complaint, I loved those kids, but it took extra work to be sure everyone was working to the best of their abilities while not interfering with the abilities of others to work.

If you're interested in being student-centric, your classroom involves a lot of trial and error. If you're not and would rather be teacher-centric, it's much easier. You teach the way that best works for you, and the kids try to keep up. You don't adapt, you expect the kids to adapt. You justify this attitude with, "In the Real World™ students won't have someone catering to their specific needs and they should learn that now. I'm helping them get stronger. They are welcome." You don't have to learn to dance to a variety of beats because the kids should learn the specific step you're teaching them and follow along to your song.

It might be clear now how I feel about this kind of teaching. It is easier though. For the teacher. Not so much for the learners.

I want a student-centric classroom. I want students to have as much control as possible over the class and their learning. It's important to me that my students learn skills that will serve them far beyond my classroom, while also learning the material I am charged with teaching. It took my student teacher and I a long time to find ways to get to a point that kind of learning worked for most of our class, because it involves a lot of freedom, and they did not always make the best choices. They were a noisy, easily distracted bunch. My go-to advice for a teacher of a noisy class is, "Give them something interesting to talk about. Don't waste time trying to silence them." So we did. We worked together every day to plan engaging, interesting lessons and projects. We incorporated movement and games. We had plenty of one-on-one and whole-group conversations about expectations and used positive reinforcement as often as we could.

Boy, did the class struggle anyway.

It was more than just being chatty. Most of the class talked all the time. While I was teaching. While my student teacher was teaching. And especially outside of our classroom, when they were with the PE, Music, or Library teachers. That's worse that being chatty with me. How students act in my room is one thing, but when they are out and about, representing our room, I have high expectations. I don't expect unquestioning, robotic obedience. I do expect the most on-top-of-it, well-behaved class that teacher sees that day.

Maybe it wasn't most of the class. It probably wasn't. That happens in a classroom. It becomes easy to focus on the three or four or five students making poor choices, and you accidentally start lumping in the whole class with them. What are the odds that I got 36 talkative, disrespectful students? Zero chance. But in the midst of the year it's easy to get tunnel vision. My student teacher and I were having to constantly re-evaluate and discuss where the struggles were and where the highlights were.

Part of this constant re-evaluation process is making sure you don't label the struggling kids as Troublemakers. Choose not to do this, because you're painting with a broad brush that isn't fair. Do I actually have five troublemakers, or do I have five kids whose needs are not being met satisfactorily? Five kids who are acting out because they aren't getting what they need? One of the best parts of an IEP meeting (student teachers- prepare to sit in All The Meetings, and IEP meetings are big ones. Mentor teachers- bring your student teacher to All The Meetings), is when you're asked to list the student's strengths. You will have students that will make your mind go blank for the briefest of moments when asked that question. It doesn't make you a bad person, assuming you notice that blank and realize that's a problem. It means that you've been focused so much on "the problem" that you've temporarily forgotten you're dealing with a small human who needs us to see all sides and encourage them first. You are always on your student's side. I had a kid who would toss her hair, roll her eyes, and tell me she hated me and school and everyone else with that *tone* kids can affect. Still on her side. Still sometimes needing to count to five and take a breath, but still on her side. She's not a troublemaker, she's having trouble. How can I help?

The large classroom meant that there were many students who needed us to think more specifically about their needs. Now, every student needs that, but some need it more to be successful. Equity not equality. Behaviors stem from needs. Teaching is juggling needs. We had a lot of flaming torches in the air. (I told you before, I can't say, "We had a lot of balls in the air." Recess duty ruined me. I only play a mature adult on TV.)

My room is set up in such a way that students should feel the freedom in the air. Choice of seats, lots of time to talk, lots of group work, lots of choice in how projects and assignments are done. A controlled space, but with wide open areas and lots of trust. I start from a place of trust, rather than make students earn it. I expect the students to trust me right off the bat. Why? Because I'm a teacher? That's not a good enough reason. Authority alone does not beget trust. Yes, this attitude has gotten me in trouble. Doesn't make it untrue. Probably makes it more true. Yes, it's a little ironic that a teacher has a strong anti-authority streak, since I'm employed as the first example of The Man most people will meet. But I get to teach kids to question authority, including mine. If a teacher's authority can't withstand questioning from a ten year old, it's not actually authority. Start from trust, eventually it will run in both directions.

Our class, in ways big and small, took advantage of that trust. Not all the kids, but enough. There's a forest fire effect that happens in classrooms sometimes, where kids who would never be disrespectful follow the lead of others who are, and suddenly a series of small things become a Big Thing. That turns the teacher into a fire fighter, and I hate being a firefighter. Sparks all over the classroom mean you're running over here to put out this fire, then running over there to put out that fire, then back again. All the while this inattention is causing more sparks to jump and fires to spread. In the middle of all this there are always those students who just want everyone to get along and everything to be fine, but it gets harder and hard for their peers to hear them over the bucket brigade. I want to say that it can happen to the best of us because it happened to me, but instead I'll just say that it happened to me and leave it at that.

It happened to me with a student teacher, no less. Not only am I concerned about teaching and reaching these kids, but I'm also trying to be sure my student teacher is getting what she needs and seeing things that she can use later in life. I'm being even more reflective and open about my process, to her and to our students, than I would normally have been. I am open and honest with the students, too. Teaching is not a magic show, it's not against the rules to show the students how the tricks work. They love seeing that, it makes them feel even more a part of the room because then they're backstage making the show go, not in the audience watching it happen. So we'd talk about how they were feeling and how I was feeling. The class got really good at the Serious Reflective Conversation script. Especially after repeated struggles with substitutes.

"We're sorry. We were wrong. It shouldn't have happened. We were disrespectful." I wasn't holding up cue cards and I wasn't telling them what I wanted to hear, but they knew it. Ever do that thing to your parents where you say what you know they're driving at during a lecture to try and get ahead of them and end the lecture faster? It was that. But that's all it was for too many of them. At some point, and I told them this too, words are just words. We needed to do better.

So we'd reset. We'd talk about how we could be better together. We co-wrote a Class Agreement, detailing what our class norms and expectations are. Norms, for those of you lucky enough to have never heard this CorporateSpeak, means the expected behaviors and rules. In a business meeting the norms might be, "We'll all be on time. Conversations will stay on topic. No texting." Our class built something like this. I thought having it clearly written and displayed in black and yellow (white poster paper is boring) would help. We all signed it.

It worked for two weeks.

In all of this my student teacher was right there with me, working alongside me to find ways to help our kids be successful. I want to stress this- we weren't looking for newer and more creative punishments. We were looking for solutions. We'd bounce ideas off each other. We'd research what others had done and discuss how to adapt those strategies for our class. The struggle helped our working relationship.

It came to a head right before spring break. The class had a few really bad days with a substitute while I was out of state. Bad days like I got an email from the sub when I was in the airport and it ruined my flight home bad days. I had one of those conversations (ok, this one was a monologue, because I just could not at that moment) with my class I'll never be happy about. I was louder than I should have been, and more emotional than I should have been. I didn't cross any lines and wasn't unprofessional, but I wasn't the best I could be either. I felt like I was a bad model for my kids and for my student teacher. I knew something needed to change because we'd never last this way. I'd lost the ability to find positive things. I try to run my class using a 5:1 ratio. Five positive comments for every one negative. I don't keep specific count, but you can tell when you're hitting your mark and when you're not. I hadn't forgotten the ratio, I just stopped using it. I found myself looking for things to correct instead of things to praise. That should always throw up a red flag in your brain. Our job is not to catch kids making the wrong choice. We're not cops. It was a bad time all around.

I was so bad, in fact, that I did something I'd never done before- with my student teacher in tow, I went to my principal, sat down in her office, and said, "We've tried x, y, and z and we're all out of ideas. Please help. What do you have?" I've never *ever* said this to a principal. I've never had one I trusted that much. I've never had one I thought could give me the kind of actionable feedback we needed right then. My willingness to do this says a lot about how good of an administrator she is.

I really did need the help. But I also did it because I wanted my student teacher to see that asking for help isn't a bad thing. The goal is to find ways to best help the students in the classroom, regardless of how uncomfortable and insecure it makes you. It's not a great feeling, going to your boss and asking for help like that. A bad administrator will hold that over your head forever and it'll show up on evaluations as a negative. A good administrator will help and will appreciate you having the self-awareness to know you need it. Our administrator took our concerns seriously, gave them thought, gave us some strong advice. Then off to spring break we went.

I spent the first few days of break not thinking about teaching. I played video games, played with my kids, read, tried to nap, anything to flush the system clean. This is important, student teachers. You will want to be The Best Teacher All The Time. You will want to buy into the narrative that teachers are always thinking about teaching and if you love your kids you're always doing whatever you can to be better for them. Well, sometimes that means not thinking about them. That means going as far from teaching as possible and decompressing. Our love for our students is used as a weapon against us all the time. You will be in the middle of a contract negotiation and you'll hear a friend, relative, or media person say, "If these teachers loved their students they'd do this for free." It'll be used to make you feel worse for talking strike or demanding better pay and working conditions. It's not fair and it's not right. A happy teacher is a better teacher. Burnout is a danger and self-care is important. Never feel bad about taking time to yourself, not being at school until dark, or reading books that aren't written by someone with a

PhD. Rest is when muscles get stronger. This is a hard job, and we deserve to lighten the load when we can. It's not being a bad teacher to step away on breaks. Be a human. Be a people. This will make you a better teacher.

Once I'd felt like I'd cleaned out my system and gotten some rest, I had my student teacher over to the house and we spent a few hours hammering out something new. As the mentor teacher, it was my job to have ideas when she got there. I had three plans of action, mapped them out for her, and together we chose one to go with.

We decided on a class economy. I'd never done a class economy before. I'd thought about it, and I'd admired teachers who had a working class store and bank. That is an impressive amount of organization. Too much organization for me, or so I thought. A class economy, complete with jobs, salaries, taxes, and items and abilities for purchase, checked all the boxes we felt we needed and had been lacking. Carrying classroom money around meant that we had an in-hand, concrete way to positively reinforce behaviors. The goal was to give more money than we took away. The money wasn't to be used for learning goals, just behavior. I resisted early in the planning stages because I didn't want to tie anything to money, I like intrinsic motivation. But it's nonsense to think that intrinsic motivation is the only thing kids need. Repeat after me: **The only thing to be hardline about in education is not being hardline about anything**. There is no other ONLY. There is no other NEVER. There is what works. I got over myself, and we got to work for our kids.

We took away all the alternative seating and fancy desk options and made kids buy their ways back to them. This meant there was a consequence, but students had choice and agency about when that consequence ended. We came up with a list of other things, both individual and whole class, that could be bought. We created a class bank account that was separate from individual accounts. The whole class got money for whole class things- transitions, compliments from other teachers, etc- which they could spend on not having assigned seating any more, not having a specific line order any more, getting the class puppets back, and so on. One interesting result of this was that they never chose to buy back line order choice. For context- I let my students line up in whatever order, same theory as the seating charts one. I trust you, it's a line, you can do this, let's not make it harder than it needs to be. This class had too many students who put talking to friends above the needs of the group, so my student teacher drew up a specific line order. During one of our class meetings a student said that when they had a specific order they did better in line, they lined up quicker and quieter at recess and lunch, and were overall more successful. The rest of the class agreed with her. I was not expecting that, but it was the kind of group understanding I'd hoped would come from the change. Students were also able to take money from their own accounts and donate it to the class account, called the Toof Trust after one of our class monster puppets. All of this was aimed at improving our class environment, how we worked as a whole and interpersonally.

And it worked.

It never would have worked without my student teacher. She had a better mind for organization than I do and she helped keep me on track with it. This kind of a program doesn't work if you're not consistent. A change has to feel real to students to matter. You can't do something for a day or two, decide it's not working, and toss it out. You need to be willing to toss it out, but you've also got to be willing to let to live for a while first, and change it as you go. Classroom programs should adapt and evolve because a classroom is a living ecosystem.

There were things about the class economy that didn't work right away, and my student teacher and I talked through how to change them and make them work. Then we'd talk to our class about the changes and get their feedback. Class ownership was vital. If the kids don't buy-in, nothing will work.

By completely taking our discipline plan and class environment apart and putting it back together, my student teacher and I saved our school year. Earlier in the year we'd started the process by blending our lessons. A blended lesson is when you make a video of the teaching, kids watch the video, and then do the assignment. It's better than listening to a lecture because they can pause, go back, re-watch, and learn at their own pace. It also means we can walk the room and help more effectively. The class as a whole wasn't handling more traditional lessons well, so this change helped us. The class economy helped us.

Having a student teacher is no reason to not try new things. In fact, it's a great reason to try new things. Ask for help, rebuild, try, try again. Student teachers should see that a classroom is not an unassailable edifice. It's a living thing. It grows, it changes, it evolves. A classroom adapts to the needs of the students and teachers within it. Students first, but if the room isn't working for you as a teacher that's still a problem. A classroom is where everyone lives, and it should be a place of safety and happiness for everyone.

Mentor teachers- don't be an unchanging rock. Be a people.

Let your student teacher see your struggle and your process to solving the struggle. Students should not be given assignments to which there is only one path to success. A classroom does not have one path to success. My student teacher that year saw three or four variations on a classroom, and for that she's a stronger teacher. She knows she doesn't have to be right right away. She has to be moving towards right. She has to keep in mind that her students come first and their needs matter. It is our job as teachers to make a space that kids can learn in. Students should meet us halfway and try, yes. It makes the job easier. It's great when they do. But that's not their job. Their job is to learn, ours is to find ways to help them learn.

I encourage mentor teachers to help student teachers find their own paths as well. I involve my student teachers in everything that happens in our classroom. Her name is on the letters home, and I insist she's in the class picture, because this is a joint effort. Make sure your student teacher feels like a valued voice. Just because they're new doesn't mean they don't have good ideas. No one should be made to sit down, shut up, and follow along. That's not good teaching, good leading, or good mentoring. Make them a part of the process, but then encourage them to find their own process.

Learning and teaching are journies. We're all headed towards similar goals, but there are infinite ways of getting there. Part of being a mentor teacher is allowing your student teacher to find ways that work for them in a safe environment where they can experiment, make mistakes, modify, and go again.

Student teachers- be a part of the process, not apart from it. Don't waste this chance. Don't take it for granted. Don't passively wait to be asked. Have a voice. Have opinions. A good mentor teacher will respect that. You have value, add it to your classroom and your school.

I think about Swamp Castle from **MONTY PYTHON AND THE HOLY GRAIL**. "They said I was daft to build on a swamp, but I built it all the same. That sank into the swamp. So I build another one. That sank into the swamp. So I built a third one! That burned down, fell over, then sank into the swamp. But the fourth one, that stayed up." Classrooms and lessons are often castles built on swamps. Good ones stay up because they're built on the ruins of failed ones. Teach student teachers to rebuild. Then someday all this can be yours.

...no, not the curtains.

16. What's Your Story Part 2

Remember What's Your Story Part 1 from before? That, but more. The more stories you have to fall back on, the fewer mistakes you have to make for yourself. And when you make those mistakes anyway, you'll know that other teachers did it too and survived. As with the first What's Your Story chapter, the stories are uncut, and I have not added my own commentary. The reason for this is, I believe the stories speak for themselves, and I want you, the smart, savvy reader, to draw your own conclusions and learn your own lessons. That will be more powerful than anything I could add.

Rusul Alrubail - Executive Director of The Writing Project

My student-teaching experience happened when I was doing my MA program in Literature. Graduate students were given an opportunity to take on a teaching-assistant contract to teach university undergraduates under the guidance of a professor. We were in charge of running the seminars that occurred after the lectures, and we were also in charge of marking.

Throughout my role as a teaching assistant that year, I learned that teaching assistants were not only important to help professors mark and do a lot of the grunt work in terms of office hours, and meeting with students one-on-one. Teaching assistants actually were an important part of humanizing the learning experience for university students.

My professor was very rigorous. I remember two weeks before I started the MA program I got an email from her with a huge package that we needed to go through as TA's. She was apparently different from the other professors that my fellow peers were working with. She had high expectations and let you know about them beforehand. I was very intimidated. I was in fact terrified. It would've been my first time teaching in a classroom, and much less, teaching adults!! Can I do it and still do all the work she expected of me?

My most memorable experience was when she came in to observe one of my seminars. I prepared the students from the day before. We were studying poetry, which is often a hard topic to teach, because students don't usually enjoy it. I gave my handouts and discussed the goal of the seminar for 10 minutes. After that I led the class to have a discussion about the poem. I don't recall exactly what poem it was at the time, but I created questions that can help students to relate the theme of the poem to modern day issues.

Students participated and engaged very well throughout the entire seminar, and I had a feeling that they did because she was also their professor and they wanted to impress her.

What's memorable about that seminar was her feedback to me. Overall it was positive, and the one thing that was constructive to my teaching career was regarding interacting with students' comments and discussion points. She said: *when a student gives you their opinion or answer to the discussion question, try to expand on it with your own to extend the conversation, but without diverting from the topic.* This suggestion was very useful for me when I became a professor myself in the classroom, and felt that when I applied it, it helped my discussions to thrive and develop into strong conversations.

She taught me that students need to feel that their opinion matters by seeing other relate to it. Connecting with others, especially students by extending the conversation and moving the discussion forward gives us an opportunity to expand on each other's thinking to grow from the conversation.

William Chamberlain- Jr High social studies

At the time I thought my student teaching experience was pretty great. I had the support of a wonderful supervising teacher and principal and, although I made lots of mistakes, they continued to support me. Unfortunately, it turns out I was wrong.

Looking back with twenty plus years of experience I realized there was one glaring problem with my student teaching experience- me. I was cocky, self assured, and absolutely ready to graduate and get my first job. I was clueless.

I was an easy student growing up. I rarely had to work to pass a class and to be brutally honest I don't work hard at anything I don't have a real interest in. I could pretty much sleep through class and still pass. I treated my student teaching experience the same way.

I have learned from a lot of conversations that it often seems to be very difficult to transition from a 'good' student to a good teacher. I know personally I struggled with empathising with struggling students. I found them frustrating. What comes easy to me should come easy to everyone, right?

Fortunately with experience (and those painful but valuable conversations with other teachers) I finally realized that my student teaching experience was indicative of my student and teaching experience and that I needed to change a lot of things if

I were ever going to become a good teacher. So, my advice is to walk into student teaching humbly. Recognize that the easy things may be a liability and not a strength. Find mature teachers and ask them a lot of 'why' questions and push them to explain to you in words you can understand and ***listen*** to them.

Sarah Windisch- Music

Kevin sat at his desk, hands folded calmly, Perfectly Neutral Teacher Face™ on, breathing slow and deliberate.

Not me. I was livid. In fact, I'm nearly positive that if I'd been any hotter we'd have all been outside in the snow because I'd set off the fire alarm. The look on that kid's face. The tone of his voice - even now, 15 years later, I still get mad at those three little words: "You wouldn't dare."

Oh, yes I would, young man.

See, there was a sixth grade class at the school where I student taught that was hilarious and awesome, but had no idea where The Line was. As both a tuba player and human with the personality of a junior high boy, I understand this struggle well, and naturally got along smashingly with this class. I was, in my humble opinion, helping them master the supremely important life skill of tiptoeing right up to The Line without crossing it. That was, until He moved in.

Kid was coolness defined. Steps and sweet kicks, slang that was new to us - the kids adored him.

I found him intimidating.

And he knew it.

As you can imagine, I lost the class then. The behavior, the relationship - gone. That's how we wound up with me barely containing my rage at being challenged by an 11-year-old, my mentor teacher looking on, and the entire class getting disciplinary referrals. Every one of them. Some of the students in the class had never had one. And these referrals - pink slips as they were known - were serious business. They weren't taken lightly by anyone. I pulled out the nuclear option...on the entire class.

After I cried in the bathroom for half an hour, I had to face my mentor teacher, the classroom teacher, and the principal to explain why 26 kids now had pink slips. I didn't have the best reason - I'd lost my cool and needed to find a way to make myself back into an authority, and in the heat of the moment, I'd said they were all getting them. What my supervisors saw though, was that I said I was going to do something (even something extreme) and then followed through. My mentor teacher and principal supported me completely, even if they didn't agree with what I'd done.

So here's the moral, and it's not "don't punish the whole class" because on occasion, you really do need to. We all need to think before speaking, because as teachers, we have to be prepared to follow through on anything and everything we say. As student teachers, this is a skill we're learning - by doing, and as mentor teachers, this is a skill we need to support and model, complete with all its consequences.

Josh Stumpehorst- Learning Commons Director

It was the best of times, it was the worst of times. It was student teaching.

I vividly remember somewhere around my fourth day of student teaching when my cooperating teacher stepped out of the room never to be seen from again. Yes, he would drop in from time to time, but essentially I was on my own without a clue in the world as to what I was doing. To say I had a baptism by fire would be an understatement for sure. At the time I remember being incredibly frustrated and often voiced this with my fellow student teachers back in the college dorms. Many of them told stories about this great bond they were building with their cooperating teacher or how they were such a tight team. I, on the other hand, was left to fend for myself in a classroom of puberty stricken 7th graders.

While being left on your own so early in a teaching experience may sound nightmarish, it was actually a blessing in disguise. I was forced to figure it out. I had to navigate the behavior problems, parents, grading, lessons planning, and everything else that goes with the job. Lots of student teachers are forced to fall lock-step in with their cooperating teachers and teach like them. Some are given so little autonomy they really don't have a true teaching experience. Despite being left to my own devices, I was actually able to build my own teaching style and techniques. I really didn't know how to do everything which allowed me to try anything. So while I was upset initially with being left alone, I truly believe it forced me to become independent and therefore a more confident and capable teacher early in my career.

Patrick Harris- 1st Grade Teacher

The Michigan winter didn't stop me from arriving at my placement school on time. It was my first day. Though I was exhausted from the lack of sleep and the egregious amount of homework from my college classes, I was looking forward to being able to impact students who looked like me and came from the same background I did. When I walked into the elementary school, I was greeted by tiny hands waving towards me. My third-grade students were transitioning from the lunchroom to continue their day of learning. Their teacher was tall and large. Her hair was blonde and grey-streaked. She took big steps when she led the line. She had her finger on her lip and made her eyes big to remind students that they should be silent. Everyone was silent, except Deshaun.

I stood in the back of the room. I was still in the observing phase of student teaching. I watched students fidget. I watched them have conversations with their neighbors about what they had for dinner the night before and their plans for after school. Their faces smiled. Some students mischievously poked fun with the students at their table. Mrs. Jackson would stare at students tell they felt her glare on their shoulders.

Mrs. Jackson announced that they were going to practice writing paragraphs. She plopped at her desk, shoveling through papers to get to her document camera. The students gripped their pencils and copied the board, all students except Deshaun. Deshaun had mahogany skin and high-top fade with a star drawn in the back. He was taller than most of the kids in his class. His pants sagged and his uniform shirt reached his knees. Certainly, by the lowering of his eyes and his ability to balance a pencil on his middle finger showed how interested her was in the lesson.

Mrs. Jackson peeked over her stack of papers and halted the class to correct Deshaun. "Pick up your pencil. Shut your mouth. Turn your eyes to the board." Deshaun picked up his pencil, kept his mouth shut and turned his eye to the board.

I stood behind Mrs. Jackson because that's where she said I'd have the best observation view. She leaned over to me as she wrote under the camera to whisper a secret in my ear. "See, Deshaun, he can't read. He's two grade levels behind. I'm not going to push him in writing. But, I will for math. He's going to be a great factory worker one day."

A factory worker? My gut bubbled. The hair on the back of my neck stood straight. I stood there with my arms folded and my lips tight. The lesson continued.

Students were nearing the conclusion sentence of their teacher-written paragraph. Deshaun pencil twirled on his desk. He had written a few words but it did not match the exemplar response. Mrs. Jackson was still behind her desk. Her slouch deepened after she marked each period. The door opened. It was the teacher from next door, Mr. Cromey. The class waved and shouted his name in excitement, except Deshaun.

Mr. Cromey, stood tall with, grey pants, a white dress shirt, tucked, and a loosened blue necktie. He high fived Mrs. Jackson at her desk. Their white hands grasped and Mrs. Jackson pulled Mr. Cromey to whisper gossip in his ear. The crowd was getting restless. Suddenly, the entire room freezes.

"Stop Deshaun!" screeched Tina. All eyes pointed towards Tina. You could hear her burettes shake. Mrs. Jackson and Mr. Cromey both turned red.

"Deshaun again?" Mrs. Jackson yelled.

"Deshaun again." Mr. Cromey echoed.

"He's been doing this all day."

"I'm not surprised."

"And I bet if you looked at his paper…"

"It won't be right!" The both said.

Deshaun twirled his thumbs and looked at them both.

"Leave me alone." Deshaun finally spoke.

My eyes lit up in astonishment and admiration.

"Excuse me?" Mrs. Jackson finally stood. Mr. Cromey moved towards Deshaun. The class was quiet.

"Yes, excuse me son?" Mr. Cromey echoed. Mr. Cromey snatched Deshaun's paper ripping horizontally. He pieced it together with his hand and announced to the class that his paper was a non-example.

"And, he's talking back! No respect for authority." Mrs. Jackson bounced over to Mr. Cromey's side.

"And he's talking back."

"And we ought to call your father for your disrespectful mouth and your unruly behavior. It's despicable!"

Deshaun looked at the both of them. He stared. The room was dead silent. My hand was on the top of my head.

"You can't call my daddy cause my daddy in jail." Deshaun responded and then he clinched his fist. You could see Mr. Cromey gulp the spit in his mouth.

"Well, we'll call your mother. It's that simple!" Mrs. Jackson responded with a fierceness. Mr. Cromey nodded his head in agreement.

Deshaun's head smacked the desk. I finally spoke. I volunteered to take Deshaun outside of the classroom. I patted him on the back and asked him to come with me. He stood up and took one final look at the teachers and walked out with me hand in hand.

We took a slow stroll through the hallways. His head was down. I took my finger and pushed it up. My mind was racing of the perfect things to say. I had nothing.

"Well, what do you want to be when you grow up?" I asked.

"A football player." Deshaun responded.

"Wow. Have you started practicing?" "My mom put me on a team."

"Hey! That's cool! I know you will make your dad proud."

He looked up at me.

"Have you read any books about football players?"

"No." Though his answers were short his tone lightened.

"I got you."

"Thanks." He gave me a thumbs up.

"Hey. Um. Don't let those teachers get to you. I know that's sort of a hard thing to say to a third grader but it's worth saying. If nobody has your back, I do. I will help you when you get frustrated. I will help you when you get stuck. I will push you when you accomplish your goal and then push you to the next one. I got your back."

"Thanks." He gave me another thumbs up.

We were back at the doors. The students were still writing their paragraph. His ripped paper hung off the corner of his desk.

"You ready?"

He sighed and then turned the knob. We both entered the classroom.

17. I Don't Know If This Is Good Advice

A student teacher I had made a habit of writing down some of the nonsense I said during the year that made her laugh. I guess there was a lot of it. There's one that stood out to her, and when she brought it up later, it stood out to me too. It's a belief I have that I doubt is popular in teaching circles and one that would probably get people fired up at me if they heard me say it. But that doesn't make me believe it's any less true.

"I don't know if this is good advice or not, but during your first and second years you're not going to get to them all. Some kids are not going to get what they need despite your best efforts. Accept that, while still struggling to prove me wrong."

Teachers aren't supposed to be defeatist. I will spend an entire year with a student teacher telling her or him how awesome they'll be in their own room. I believe that, I wouldn't say it if I didn't.

I also believe those first years are harder than you can imagine. A good teacher wants to give every single student everything they need. A good teacher is invested in the learning of anyone who enters their classroom. A good teacher takes a student's learning personally. We can't help it.

But there is so much to education that isn't teaching. That's the hard stuff. The meetings and tests and hoops. Going to professional developments run by people who haven't internalized their own topic. "Direct lecture is bad for learning and I have 156 slides to prove it." Juggling the hundred different things that come up during the school year that draw focus away from where it should be. These put stressors on veteran teachers. For brand new teachers, this can be overwhelming.

Mentor teachers, I ask again- make your student teacher a part of every single thing that happens at your school, no matter how big or small. They should be prepared for all the ancillary jobs that go along with being a teacher. It shouldn't be a shock to their systems that first year when they're all alone. Immunize them.

Student teachers- it'll still be a shock. A mentor teacher, even a good one that lets you have freedom, acts as a buffer. There's mental shielding that happens, where part of your brain tells you, "Wow, that's a lot of stuff he's got to do. Glad he's the teacher and not me." You could be thinking this even as you're getting your hands dirty right alongside your mentor teacher. It's different when the chair is yours alone.

Because of that, and because there will be so many students with so many needs, you will watch as some slip away. You'll swim against the tide and struggle as hard as you can but there is so much to do and only so much that can be done. You will lose that first year. You will also win. You will have many successes, but any one loss makes that hard to see. It's similar to performing on stage. If I'm running a professional development and telling jokes and the whole room is laughing and with me except for one guy sitting way in the back corner of the room, he's all I'll be able to think about. I'll finish the session consumed by that one guy. Why didn't he laugh? The classroom is that but over and over every day. Most of my students excelled and learned. How could I never reach that one kid?

As you student teachers grow and become better teachers,

you'll find ways to reach more and more students. Your box of tricks will deepen and fill. Your bandwidth will increase, and those Teacher Senses I talked about will continue to strengthen. Students won't get away as often because you'll know how to be proactive and you'll know quicker ways to reach them. These are things that can only come with time.

I'm not telling you this so you have an excuse in your pocket. Don't miss a kid and pull this chapter out and wave it around, "Doug said this would happen!" I'm not telling you to look at your first class and think, "This kid. He's the one I'm not going to catch." It's not a goal. It's an accident that happens despite best efforts. I'm telling you so that when you're feeling down on yourself, in your room after all the students have gone, wondering what you've done wrong and why you aren't better, you can read this and know that this job is unlike any other and the pressure we put on ourselves is a pressure few others can understand. Teaching is a long game, and we only get to see a short bit of it. Sometimes you'll feel as though you failed a student, unaware of the impact you made because you're blinded by what you Think you needed to do rather than seeing what you actually Did.

Still try. Forget Yoda. That little green Muppet only had one student at a time. Sometimes there's a try. Break your tail trying to reach everyone. Remember that teaching is a profession we grow into. I think back on my first two classes and shudder. You know that old joke about feeling good, sliding into bed, comfy under the covers and ready to sleep, when suddenly your brain says, "Hey, remember that super embarrassing thing you did six years ago? Let's relive that in agonizing detail over and over, shall we?" Teaching does not make sleep come any easier some nights, no matter how tired you are. I want to find kids from my early classes and apologize, "I'm sorry, I was doing my best but I didn't know what I was doing." Heck, there are still students I had that I want to grab on the first day of the following year and pin a note to their shirts before sending them to their new teacher, "I tried. I could have done better. This is a great kid. Sorry."

Teachers can use failure as fuel. Anger and failure don't burn as cleanly or for as long as better motivators like hope, joy, and love, but they'll get you off the ground and moving. Only if you don't internalize the struggle, if you turn it outwards and use it to propel you forward. Only if it brings into sharper focus that what's most important at that point is to be better for the next class.

You won't catch every kid that first year. You will use that to constantly get better. I don't know if it's good advice, but I'm going to say it anyway.

To end this chapter on a lighter note, here's the complete list of things that came out of my face that my student teacher Veronica thought were worth writing down in the back of her journal. I'll add context if I have any idea what context there could be-

- *"That's a thing you can do...use your students to make up with your parents. Write that down."* I call my parents on their birthdays from my classroom and have my students sing Happy Birthday to them. Parents love this, they think it's cute. It's like buying a gift, but cheaper. Note- does not work on significant other.
- *"That's the dumbest f**king Hallmark card sh*t."* I have strong opinions about meaningless cotton candy phrases

that are thrown at teachers as a way to sound deep. Teaching is too often oversimplified or trivialized by those trying to sound smart, and it drives me around the bend. I swear this was not said to or in front of students.

- *"Dirt's different than people."* I have no idea what I was talking about, but I stand by it.
- *Me on a hot day: "It's getting hot in hurr." Student with extreme side-eye: "Don't ever ever use that phrase."* It's fun to pretend to be hip and with it. That's my only excuse.
- *"I bet your classmates' mentor teachers don't cuss this much."* This is a true statement.
- *"Seriously, you guys? You don't know how baseball works? Terrible children."* For the record, I don't make a habit of calling my students terrible. They knew it was a joke, we were all laughing. This happened during a kickball game when over half the class didn't know how to play. It was unfair of me to blame the kids for not knowing. I should have said, "Terrible parents." (This is also a joke.)
- *"Don't organize and plan the way I do. I can get away with it because I've been teaching for eleven years, and it's still irresponsible."* I work hard to be sure my student teachers know there are lots of ways to teach, and I think hyperbole is the greatest thing ever.
- *"Walmart has everything except self-respect. Hahaha."* Pretty sure this wasn't said in front of students, I think she was asking where to get a specific school supply. It cracks me up that she decided she had to write down that I made myself laugh.
- *"I would kill a hobo for a projector mounted on the ceiling."* Murder is wrong. But so is not having projectors

mounted on the ceiling. That's all I'm saying. Also not said in front of students.

➢ *"Any project or lesson that ends with the kids asking to do it again is a good project or lesson."* Hey look, she wrote down good advice too!
➢ *"What kind of adoptions do you have? Like, what kind of puppies."* Listen- meetings about adopting new curriculum are long, ok?
➢ *"We must go puppet shopping!"* This is always true. Kids love puppets. Teach with puppets.
➢ *"Every single one of these makes me sound awful out of context."* This is the text I sent to her after she sent me this list.
➢ *"My dad thought they were hilarious."* The text she sent back.

18. Going It Alone

As the school year progresses the burden of responsibility should shift from mentor teacher to student teacher. This includes all responsibilities that can be reasonably transferred, from planning and teaching lessons to creating projects to Those Conversations with students. Student teachers should take over all of it.

To be specific- student teachers should take over all of it, while still under the eye of their mentor teacher. After all, mentor teachers, at the end of the day those are our students. My name is on the lease. There's a difference between stepping away and hiding in the teacher's lounge.

Every university program has their own timetable and way of doing things. When I was a mentor teacher in Hawaii my student teachers' schedules had them moving towards taking over 100% of the classroom, at which point they soloed for two weeks. During those two weeks I wasn't even supposed to be in the room. I'd meet with my student teacher before school each day, be sure everything was good to go, answer any last minute questions and give any last minute advice, meet the kids at the door, take roll, and then I was off to the back of the library for the next few hours. At the end of the two weeks we gradually shifted most of the teaching responsibility back to me. Or we would have if we followed their directions exactly. In reality, we turned the classroom into a co-teaching situation.

The program my student teachers in Oregon went through was different in that the student teacher never officially solos.

The shift still happens, but the expected teaching breakdown, according to the program, stops at around 80/20. Because I'm bad at directions, I still push this closer to 90/10. I never stepped away from the room for any length of time. This was school policy as well as university policy. I did sneak away for longer and longer bathroom breaks though, because it's important that a student teacher be completely alone with the students. It's a different feeling when you're alone. Did I mention before that a benefit of having a student teacher is not having to wait until recess or lunch to pee? (Don't use a student teacher as an excuse to hit the copy room and make a billion copies though.)

Every mentor teacher does this shift of responsibility differently. I think of a student teacher's year as going from having never ridden a bike to doing a century (100 mile) ride. We start with observation and training wheels. Mentor teachers-we're the training wheels. When we ("we" in this case being the mentor teacher/student teacher team) think the student teacher is ready the mentor teacher steps a little further away. This is the equivalent of the parent taking off the training wheels and running alongside the bike, holding the seat and shouting encouragement. The student teacher chooses the lessons they will teach according to their specific needs and the assignments from the university. The mentor teacher is right there alongside, like a shadow. We are letting the student teacher ride, but we're sure to be there for the catch if the wobbles get too wobbly. At some point, the student teacher is riding well enough that we're able to get our own bikes out of the garage, and that's when the relationship gets really fun. There's enough trust that we are riding together. Instead of the student teacher teaching and the mentor teacher observing, we're actually co-teaching. I take a group over there, you take a group over here. We teach the same lesson to different levels of students. I run this station and you circulate and help as needed. At this point, the mentor teacher has total trust in the student teacher's abilities as a teacher. That doesn't mean the student teacher doesn't occasionally fall or struggle, but it's because the student teacher is riding faster, climbing bigger hills, and is tackling longer, more challenging races. We were practicing on the road and now it's time for a little off-road riding. It's time to drill those mountains. Where are the weak spots in the student teacher's teaching, because now we're acting as a coach, finding and fixing. But still off to the side. And finally, at the end of it all, the student teacher is ready for the long ride all alone. We wave from the door or our desk and watch them cycle off into the distance.

Assuming the student teacher/mentor teacher relationship is strong, this exchange of responsibilities will grow naturally. Student teachers- you *have* to take the initiative on this. You have to be asking and asking and asking to carry heavier academic loads. Mentor teachers- you *have* to be letting them. I cannot stress enough that the only way a student teacher will be prepared for their own classroom is to teach as much as possible in their placement(s).

If the student teacher is teaching as much as I suggest, universities should be underestimating how much teaching a student teacher will do over the course of the year. Their pacing plan for student teacher responsibility growth is a minimum because mentor teachers are unpredictable. Don't take it as gospel. You know who that pacing plan was written for? Everyone who ever goes through their program. Which makes it nearly useless as a document of specifics. Universities also know that many mentor teachers do not let student teachers teach as much as they should, and they hedge their bets accordingly in their pacing plans. We are changing that right here, right now. That is explicitly one of the goals of this book: To convince mentor teachers to let their student teachers teach even more than they think is needed. Because more is always needed. It's not a contest, but my student teacher will have more time in front of a classroom of kids than any other student teacher in her cohort. She will have more reflective conversation too. I want her going to her night classes and bragging to her classmates about all the time she's getting. The Beatles were great because they were geniuses, but also because they spent countless hours in The Cavern Club honing their craft before they broke through.

I move student teachers through the progression of release of responsibility as quickly as I think they can handle it. Because they can handle it. It's exactly the same as how we release responsibility to the students in our classrooms. Mentor teachers- use your judgement as a professional educator. Put trust in your student teacher.

In my room, a student teacher will spend maybe one full day observing. Any more than that is too much. They should be teaching. Very quickly I will be having my student teacher teaching one lesson a day. This starts with the morning work assignments. That gets boring fast though, and it's the shallow end of the pool teaching. I let the student teacher choose what kind of a lesson and in what subject they'll teach next. We co-plan that lesson and they execute it. Every day the student teacher is teaching, and soon the planning process becomes more and more efficient. Lessons that need to be done for the university take longer to plan because the university demands more of the lesson plans, but day-to-day lessons can become discussions and quick plans with ease. I plan each week on Thursday of the previous week. This allows me to be deep enough into the week that I know what needs to be retaught and fix my pacing, while allowing me to look into the future with an understanding of where my kids are and what they need.

I should note that these plans are always subject to change. And something always changes. That's teaching. It's responding to the needs of the students around you, including the student teacher. My student teacher is with me during these weekly planning sessions, and it is during these that we sketch out who will teach what in the coming week. While I need a day or less to prepare a lesson most of the time, because I know this material and I remember what worked from last year, a student teacher needs more time. As soon as I feel the student teacher has a feel for how I'd teach it, which is part of the daily reflections, I start handing over planning responsibility. We parallel plan a lot of the time. This means that while I'm working out most of the week, the student teacher is next to me detailing the lessons she has chosen, checking with me, asking clarifying questions, and talking to herself. Student teachers- talking to yourself is important when lesson planning. I hope. Because I do it all the time. This often leads to my student teacher looking up and saying, "What? I didn't catch that." and me replying, "Didn't catch what? Oh, I was talking to my plan book again." Yes, I still use a lesson plan book. It's one of the only parts of my teaching that hasn't gone digital. I like having the book in pen and pencil.

By making the student teacher privy to your planning practice, they will have a model to work from when you turn the ship over to them. During this phase we still parallel plan, but this time I'm checking email, doing paperwork, and filling out that form the office has been asking for for a week and a half while the student teacher is planning the whole week out. Because I'm a big believer in freedom, I will no longer be insisting that the student teacher plan the week out like I do. Earlier in the year, yes. Because I want them to have a workable template. However, I encourage student teachers to explore the world beyond our room and find a system that might appeal more to them. My way is not the only way. How much better will it be for them to find a system that works *before* stepping into their own room all alone? Answer: So much better. So as long as I understand the chosen system and I know the days are planned, I'm a happy panda (or panther or cougar or whatever the school mascot happens to be).

Student teachers- work smart during this time. There is almost never a reason to be at school until seven pm. I urge you not to become that teacher. It's how burnout happens. For some reason, parts of society lionize football coaches who spend countless hours sacrificing their lives to looking at tape and game planning. In any other job that wouldn't be called dedication, it would be called a shocking lack of efficiency. Don't sacrifice yourself on the altar of Plannicus, the teaching god of lesson planning. Plan smarter, not harder.

Also student teachers- this stage in the year is a perfect chance to work in those passion subjects you have. It's the end of the year, you have freedom, and if you're creative enough just about anything can be made to fit the standards. I'll often work backwards with standards, creating the interesting lesson first, then looking at the standards and seeing where they intersect. Well-written standards and well-written lessons work together. If you've always loved bugs or space or literature and you haven't had a chance to indulge yourself, do it now. Keep in mind that it's about the kids and their learning more than it is about you getting to teach a topic you've always wanted to teach, but we can have both things. I find excuses to talk about Shakespeare and Star Trek and the planets and movies all the time. The trick, and this is a Small Rock trick, is figuring out how to make everything mesh neatly together. You might as well start working on that now.

Along with soloing, student teachers are going to have to teach lessons on their own for their programs. Homework assignments that are actually technically classwork. Having all the time in front of the room the student teacher needs does more than make him or her more comfortable and increase their chances of success. It also prepares the students in your class and allows them to see the student teacher as s/he truly is- a teacher. You can't tell your students that the student teacher is a teacher and then never let them teach anything. Kids can see through that. The novelty of the student teacher teaching a lesson should wear off in the first week, until the kids don't even think about having a student teacher and a regular teacher. They should just think they have two teachers. The gradual transition of responsibilities will help kids adjust as well.

Students have needs that require a diverse viewpoint, so to not let your student teacher work all the time is to rob your class of value. It's often that my student teacher will see something with a student in a way I won't, or try a tack I hadn't thought of. If I've done my mentor teacher job right, the student teacher only runs these things by me after the fact because we've built the trust. I've had plenty of students who prefer the student teacher to me. It happens. They also prefer my puppets to me.

Respect the Power Dynamic

One thing not to do during the time spent as co-teachers is slip into a Good Cop/Bad Cop dynamic. When students have two teachers in the room they will try to play one parent off the other. "Mr. Robertson, can I get a computer?"

"What did Ms. Miller say?"

"She said- wait, how did you know I asked her?"

"Because I have ESP. Also, the room isn't that big and I heard you. Also also, she and I talk on a regular basis and we know you've done this before."

"Oh….so can I use a computer though?"

Mentor teachers- as the year moves forward and you start letting your student teacher have more and more time alone with the kids, it's important to respect the power dynamic you're creating in your room. You want the kids to respect the student teacher and treat her or him like a regular teacher. Which means you need to be aware of when you might be taking power aware from the student teacher without meaning to. The most obvious case of this is when you come back to the room after making copies or whatever and you find the room in a little more of a chaotic state than you'd like to see. Your Teacher Instinct will be to swoop in and demand that you Fix The Problem. Do not do this. Find your student teacher, make eye contact, use non-verbal communication to ask if they need help, then back slowly out of the room and let them fix it themselves. Sometimes they have to fail. This will lead to an excellent conversation after school. Debriefing failures is easier and more productive that debriefing success.

Once the student teacher is soloing, or whatever the university version of soloing is, it's time to cut the cord. Find something to do. I would have a conversation with my students about what's happening, but if the transition from Mostly Me to Co-Teaching to Mostly My Student Teacher has been smooth enough the kids won't even realize the hand-off has happened. After two days one will look up and say, "Mr. Robertson, did you teach us anything today?" And how you respond to that depends entirely on your definition of teaching and whether or not your name is Mr. Robertson.

I still keep my two column chart of notes, but at this point I'm probably looking at Small Rocks and specific goals. My student teacher and I are still choosing things to improve upon, but for the most part the student teacher is now simply teaching. It is at this point, more than any other up until now, that I begin to pay more attention to how the kids react than to the specifics of what the student teacher has been doing. Now, I've always been watching the kids watch, do, and learn, but my attention becomes less divided between the two. My student teacher's Teacher Senses should be becoming more acute, so they should be catching behavior cues. I'm watching for other student behaviors. This becomes instructive in my own teaching, as I'll be able to ask my student teacher, "Does he do that when I'm teaching too?" And when the answer is yes that tells me a lot.

Smartnership

Once the soloing section of the year is over, you'll be right up against the end of the year. Now you have a true teaching partner. Everything can be evenly split. The trust and relationship you've built through to this point bears fruit in the form of a smartnership that will allow you both to be even more creative with lessons. It's also a great time for your student teacher to explore other classes more freely. By now most of the university requisites will be complete or nearly complete. Wings should be spread and gaps should be filled.

Student teachers at this point often have a choice. Their program probably ends before the school year does. They'll technically need to stop coming in as often, or at all. A successful student teacher/mentor teacher relationship means that the end of the university term does not equal the end of the student teacher's time in class. The bond between student teacher and students, and student teacher and mentor teacher, will be something no one will want to give up and the student teacher will come in until the very last day.

The goal, by the way mentor teachers, on that very last day, is to get your students to make your student teacher cry. Letters of reflection work great for that. It's also a perfect chance to list on the board everything that your student teacher did with the kids over the year. That kind of concrete visual, a board full of lessons, projects, assignments, songs, dances, art, carries a lot of weight and meaning. Do this on a day your student teacher is absent at the end of the year. Trust me, they'll be exhausted or sick or both. Make them stay home to get healthy- always good advice, even in the middle of the year- and when they're home make the list. Your kids won't be able to keep it a secret for long though, because, "Miss, we have a surprise for you. It's letters!" are sentences they love to let slip out accidentally.

It's at the end of the year that the weight of what you've accomplished will hit you. You'll realize that neither of you went it alone, and together you accomplished something greater than yourselves.

19. Get a Haircut and Get a Real Job

The goal of being a student teacher is to learn enough to walk into your first job ready to rock and roll. The goal of a mentor teacher is to prepare you to do that. Which means, in my estimation, part of the mentor teacher's work is helping the student teacher actually get a job. Not just through a letter of recommendation, which should go without saying, but by stepping them through the process of convincing a principal to give an untested teacher a chance.

Putting In The Time

You want to be able to fill a résumé with accomplishments and abilities, since the Job Experience section will likely be painfully thin. That particular lack is not your fault, and administrators know that. Many won't hold a lack of experience against a new teacher. Frankly, most can't. While there are a few places where it's hard to get a job because the market is saturated and everyone wants to work there, there are many more places that need good teachers. This does not mean that you'll get a job right away. Be prepared for a job hunt. Hunts are more successful with the best possible bait.

Bait, in this case, means being able to list and talk about all the cool extracurricular work you and your mentor teacher did together. You were part of School Site Council and the MakerFaire planning committee. Alongside your mentor teacher, you were trained in that math curriculum and went to this edtech conference. You adopted puppies and fed the poor. (Note: Do not accidentally combine those two.) You volunteered to help coach the school basketball/volleyball/soccer teams. You were generally a busy little beaver in and around the school you student taught at. This tells the administrator looking over your résumé that you care about more than the classroom and that you know a teacher's day extends beyond the bells.

This is all more work on top of an already packed workload. It's also in the service of a greater good. Two greater goods, actually. The first is that you're helping the school you're working at, and schools needs all the help they can get. You're gaining experiences in meetings, which no one likes but experience breeds tolerance and an ability to learn to be successful during them. The second greater good is more meeting and committee experience means you'll have opinions in your interview, and opinions are good. You want the background to be able to make suggestions and support them in the room.

Writing It Up

I'll be honest, I write résumés based on internet templates. I don't know if there's a secret way to write one that makes it call out with a Siren song to an administrator. I do know that content matters. You did all that work during your student teaching, so write all of it down. All of it. Even the stuff that you helped with. Even the stuff that you have a passing familiarity with. Just remember- if you write it down, you had better be prepared to speak intelligently about it. Teaching has a lot in common with acting. Every single actor on the planet lists, "Horse riding," as a skill on their rèsumè. Fifteen percent of actors can actually ride a horse with any skill. But it looks good to have on there and they figure that if they do get that Western they'll have time to get a few lessons in before shooting starts. Do that, but with every single piece of technology you've ever used in a classroom.

You're not making Oscar-worthy movies, but you know how to use a movie-making program? Write it down. You know audio recording, green screen, document sharing, student engagement programs and applications? Just be able to say something pedagogical about them. I dislike buzzwords as much as anyone, but a facility with current buzzwords will make you shiny. Make a list. Mentor teachers- it's our job to prepare them, so they should have seen these things. They should have used these things. Get familiar with these things. Student teachers- try to be on the cutting edge. There is constantly some kind of new hotness in the education technology space. Figure out what it is and how it could be used in the classroom. Write it down.

A digital résumé will blow the mind of the person interviewing you. Create a website and throw links to videos of lessons you taught while student teaching on there. Link to lesson plans and images of students working on projects. Make yourself a biography page. Eyes will go wide when you ask the principal to go to your website so you can show off all the cool stuff you did with your mentor teacher. You'll be able to hear the principal think, "How many of my teachers have built their own website?"

In The Room

You got an interview. Now what?

Take a breath. Relax. Smile. Show that you're a confident person, even if you're quaking in your brand-new-just-bought-for-this-interview shoes. Project confidence and Teacher Presence. Good posture and a smile do that. This isn't in a, "Smile, sweetheart," gross way. You want to be a teacher. You love kids. You love this job. Love makes you smile. Administrators like teachers who will bring light to their school. Trust me, they've already got the Serious and the Dark Cloud positions sewn up.

Dress professionally for the job interview. Here's the rub- Teacher Professional changes by location and by gender. Speaking from my own Man Teacher experience, I always interview in a long sleeve button up, slacks, and a tie. Since wearing my hair long, I interview with it in a ponytail. Here are caveats specific to my situation that I want to make clear- I've worked in California, Hawaii, and Oregon. These are not conservative hotbeds. I have never had an administrator or parent say something negative about any of my exposed tattoos. I don't go out of my way to show them off, and in a long sleeve shirt only the one on my wrist shows. I got a job with blue streaks dyed in my hair. That administrator actually joked with me that since our school colors are purple and black, I should change the blue to purple. This is what it's like in parts of the Left Coast. I'm only bragging a little.

In conversations with teachers other places, I know that how I look is not Teacher Professional everywhere. We can have the book-by-its-cover conversation this brings up some other time. I do suggest a tie for the interview if you're a teacher candidate who identifies as male. It's pretty much all we have to do to look professional. I've only worked at one school where my principal expected a tie on the male teachers. I also worked in Hawaii for six years where shorts, an Aloha shirt, and slippahs (aka flip-flops, thongs, sandals) were ok. So my perspective on this is a little skewed. Look to your mentor teachers for their opinions on professional dress. Ideally, this has been modelled all year for you by your mentor teacher and their colleagues and it's easy to figure out.

Many teacher interviews involve a mini-lesson. Sometimes

it's a video mini-lesson, but often it's done in the room. Everyone knows this is awkward and artificial. That won't stop them. The administration and hiring team (you'll probably never interview just with a principal, there will be another teacher or two in the room a least) wants to see how you'll handle it. They also want to see what you'll do with a little freedom to impress them with a lesson. In interviews, I have been asked to teach a math lesson and a reading lesson. Both times the administrator left it open by letting me choose a lesson that fit any standard in the grade level I was interviewing for. That's nice, because then I get to deep dive into the standards and find one that plays to my strengths. As a student teacher, you'll have taught plenty of lessons by the time you're at this phase, and some will have gone better than others. Choose one that you have comfort and success with. As always, ask yourself how you can add technology or movement into the lesson. The interview team will be impressed if you tell them how you'll get the students up and moving during the lesson. If you're forced to teach the lesson in the room, go for it. Really commit. I had to teach a fractions lesson to the interviewing principal and two teachers on the interview team while we all sat around a table. It's unnatural, but that's ok. I ran with it and went through the whole spiel of how the lesson would go, I called on teachers like they were students, had them waving their hands in the air, the whole nine. If you have to do a lesson during your interview, don't do it halfway. Be brave and go all in. Do it with personality and confidence, which you'll have developed during your time student teaching, since **your mentor teacher will have been having you teach lessons on a near constant basis to prepare you**.

I'm a storyteller in interviews because I have a lot of stories that cover a wide range of situations. It's nice when a principal asks a question like, "A student is being unruly and making it difficult for others to focus on the lesson. How would you deal with this?" and I'm able to say, "That happened last year, and I did this, this, and this." Student teachers won't be able to do this in the same way, so they should be asking their mentor teachers what questions will come up in interviews, especially questions that are area- and grade level-specific. Then reflect on the year, look back through journal notes, and find real-life examples if you can. More time in front of kids, more possible real life examples to pull from. Mentor teachers- we should be role playing job interviews with our student teachers, coaching them through answers. If the student teacher has been as involved in all aspects of the school process as they should be, then they'll have many of the answers to questions they'll be asked already. If the student teacher and mentor teacher have been doing daily conversations and reflections, the student teacher will have a comfort with the educational language needed in job interviews. Talk through those special and area-specific education terms everyone hates and everyone knows. They will come in handy. This goes with acronyms too. Student teachers- know your basic educational acronyms. Use them before the interviewer does if you can to impress the interview team.

Along the same lines as using acronyms first, you're going to want to be on the bleeding edge of technology. You'll notice I've said this a few times. Might be important. If you get to teach a lesson in the room, mention an app or tool that you'll use. You get Mega Big Bonus Points if you know a educational program that the interview team doesn't. Teaching a pseudo-lesson is one thing, but having a teachable moment organically come up during an interview and getting to show off a new-to-them-old-to-you piece of edtech gets you much more than a foot in the door. How many candidates for the position will be teaching the interview team a new tool?

Do not be afraid to not know the answer to things. Teaching is a team sport, and you should know when to lean on the other members of the team. Often in interviews a question will come up that involves a specific learning disability, and part of my answer in those cases will always involve going to my special education teacher for help, or going to the school counselor. Make it clear in the interview that you aren't afraid to ask for help. It's those people's jobs to be experts. Show you understand their jobs as well as your own. Spending time as a student teacher in the special education room, the intervention room, the speech room, and so on, will give you the background you need to make these answers sing. And it'll actually be useful once you get a job. Teachers should know what everyone else's job is, otherwise you'll be in a training, someone will start talking, and you'll be leaning over to the person next to you whispering, "Yo, who the eff is this?"

At the end of every job interview the interview team asks the person being interviewed if they have any questions. You will always have questions for the interview team. You will demonstrate that you've been paying attention, and that you've done your homework. You will ask for clarification on things. You will say, "I was looking at the school website and I noticed there aren't many pictures of students using technology, what is the tech situation like here?" Then you'll follow up with questions about the schedule, how long are prep periods, are you lucky enough to have a librarian, a music teacher, a PE teacher, and so on. You can ask, "I was looking at the district site at the school's data (most every district posts test scores and the like online somewhere- find it), and I was wondering why blah blah blah." I ask about teacher autonomy because it's important to me, but I'm also a veteran teacher and know what's important to me. You'll learn the same with experience.

Should I Say Yes?

Someone once told me that dating a lot is important because it helps you build two mental lists. One list is **Things I Must Have In A Partner**. The other list is **Things I Will Not Tolerate In A Partner**. Those lists get longer and more detailed the more you date. The same is true for deciding when a school is right for you.

At first, you won't know. My best advice, when it's your first job, is to say yes to an offer unless something inside you is screaming, "SAY NO!" Make sure that voice isn't fear and isn't holding out for something even more perfect. This is true for lessons and it's true for jobs- date, don't marry. You are allowed to take a job, decide it's not the school or grade for you, and look for another one the next year, or two years on. You are never trapped in a position. Don't let yourself be. I suggest saying yes because if you say no hoping for something better to come along and nothing does you'll be the grumpiest substitute teacher in the district the next year.

But maybe you interview a bunch and nothing comes through. It could happen. Happened to me when I was starting out. Start substitute teaching. Subbing is a great learning experience. Subbing allows you to see a wide variety of classrooms, grades, and age levels. It helps you practice those discipline techniques you learned, and find out if you can engage a classroom full of students who might not be all that interested in being engaged by you. Also, and this is more of that terrible advice I shouldn't say out loud, you can have a terrible day where nothing goes right and you ruin the class for the day, and you *never have to see them again ever.* But you will have learned something valuable. As a teacher, reading that sentence terrifies me. As someone who was a sub, it's a true statement and you learn as much for those awful days as you do from the great ones.

The entire process of getting a teaching job is a strange thing because of the nature of what we do. You're asking a principal to trust you with a room full of children, and trying to convince that principal that you know what you're doing and will be capable of controlling and educating the students. You need to be able to talk technology, jargon, data, and kid equally well. Use your mentor teachers to prepare. I cannot overstate that.

Mentor teachers- this is just about the end of our job. We haven't failed if our student teacher doesn't end up hired by the next school year, there are too many factors that we have no control of. But it is quite a feeling when your student teacher bounces into the classroom or calls you on the phone bubbling over with the news that she or he got a job offer. That means, in theory, we've accomplished our goal. We prepared the student teacher well enough that someone decided they were ready to handle their own room. Our job still isn't completely over. The student teacher will have a million questions over the summer. But at that point we've moved from mentor teacher/student teacher to mentor teacher/rookie teacher. Please notice that our position hasn't changed. Once a mentor, always a mentor.

20. Small Rocks

The goal of this book is to give student teachers and mentor teachers the Big Rocks they need to have a successful year and accomplish the goals set before them. Since we're at the end of the book, we can talk about some of the Small Rock ideas of student teaching and mentor teaching.

Assault the Commonplace

Education is sometimes described as a giant ocean liner, and that's used an an excuse for why change on a large level is so difficult. It's hard to turn something so massive when it's under steam, and education is always full steam ahead. Inertia is a powerful force. Even when change is needed, wanted, warranted, and asked for, it still takes time. There are a lot of schools out there, and every one of them is filled with teachers who have their own ideas about how teaching should be done, and every one of them is a part of a district with a superintendent and a board who think they know how it should be done. That's a lot of hearts and minds.

So it's an ocean liner. Fine. Boats are built to be rocked. Small movements can cause big change. A pebble makes a ripple before the ocean liner, and however imperceptibly, that ripple does impact the liner's journey. It's good to not think about the Biggest Picture all the time, it's overwhelming. Focus on the change happening in your classrooms first. Mentor teachers- that change can be as simple as opening your door to a student teacher, and opening your mind to their new ideas. Student teachers- that change can be as simple as letting a seed of an idea grow and flower into something new, using the expertise and experience of those around you to help it bloom and spread more seeds.

Early in your career you won't be going crazy with creativity, and that's ok because you're learning the game. Once you feel you can see the Matrix code, you can start playing with it. The mainstream is shallow and easy. Go beyond it. Push yourself and our profession into new places by going there first, and then waving to everyone else. Do not accept what others say is the way teaching is done just because they say. Submit for conference sessions and spread your ideas around. Don't look at a school as an established monolith, look at it as a living creature.

I'm described as a "weird" teacher, and there's a lot of reasons for that- the puppets and hair and general sense of silliness I believe should be and is inherent to teaching and learning. But more than that, it's because I can't stand "normal." I'm not sure normal exists. I think it's just status quo. People aren't normal, people are dynamic, built to change. Don't accept what's normal.

Chekhov's Lesson Plan

Chekhov's gun is a storytelling idea put forth by Russian playwright Anton Chekhov in which he posits that if there is a gun on the wall in the first act, in the next act it should be fired. You, as an audience member, have been trained to understand this rule and certain things build anticipation within you as you watch a play, movie, or television show. You know, even if you didn't know what it was called, about Chekhov's gun. So do students.

Before a project I'll put a giant stack of cardboard on the side of my classroom. It will be there when the kids come in for the day. I won't mention it to the students. I'll let kids ask me about it, but won't give straight answers. "What giant heap of cardboard? Oh, that giant heap of cardboard? It's a giant heap of cardboard. Why is it there? The cardboard? To form the giant heap." I write a daily schedule on the board and I'll draw a giant question mark, or write the name of an activity the kids have never heard of. They'll ask, because of course they'll ask. I won't explain. I can't be subtle, but I can be coy.

By the time we get to that activity the kids are salivating for it. Imagine, a classroom full of students begging to be given an assignment. Not because I told them, "We are going to do something super awesome today!" I'm an Old, they know my idea of Super Awesome isn't their idea of Super Awesome. Instead, I let their imaginations do all the work.

As you plan lessons, keep Chekhov's lesson plan in mind. **Never do anything the kids can do for themselves.** This is true for sharpening pencils and handing out paper and it's true for building anticipation.

In Sickness

Teachers get sick. We want to push through. Writing sub plans is a pain. It's easier to come in and suffer.

Until you continue to suffer. And don't get better. And try to teach anyway. The kids need you at your best, so it's best to rest.

Mentor Teachers- student teachers will get sick. Let them stay home. Give them a day. I've sent student teachers home at recess, not because they were teaching badly or in trouble, but because I'm more concerned with their health than their reps. This is another time when letting your student teacher teach as often as possible comes in handy. Then when they do have to miss a day the percentage of instructional practice missed is relatively small. Teach your student teachers to put their health first. That includes modeling the behavior you want to see. We can't suffer through either. This is easier said than done, of course. But, if your student teacher has been teaching and knows the class and helped do the planning, then your sub plans are very simple by the middle of the year. "Student Teacher in charge. Do what she says. Have a good day. Thanks."

Cardboard

Cardboard is the most useful, versatile building material known to teachers. Stop throwing away boxes. Find a place in the classroom to stack and store it. Once you start using cardboard in class, you'll never want to stop. It's cheap, easy to get, and reusable.

Trust me- cardboard is your friend. Heavy duty tape too.

Go Outside

This is twofold, so let's do the literal one first-

Leave your classroom. Kids love field trips, but as a student teacher it's hard to plan those. You can and should suggest them if you have ideas, but it's not what I mean here. What I'm talking about is, whenever possible, leave behind the four walls of your classroom and go out of doors. There are so many lessons and projects that can be done just as well outside in the sun.

This presents a host of educational challenges. What materials will be needed? Can they hear me? How can I control my class outside? Those answers are: The simplest materials possible, clipboards are a goodness. Set the assignment up inside so you don't have to do instruction outside. If they behave for you inside, they should behave for you outside. That last one is like any other skill- it's not a real ability until it's repeatable. It will take practice for them and you. One failure does not mean stop.

Adjust your definition of suck.

Being outside wakes kids up. Anything that mixes things up is a positive. Going outside does that. Let students feels the wind in the hair and the sun on their skin. They'll be inside plenty.

There are technology considerations when doing lessons outside. Namely, I don't like my laptops leaving the room. Phones and tablets are different. As much as I love students learning with technology, it's a tool and tools should be put aside sometimes. What can be done outside that could never be done in the classroom or on a computer? Expand your horizons.

While expanding your horizons, think on the second meaning of *Go Outside*. Go outside the educational arena for inspiration. Teachers do not have a monopoly on creativity and good ideas. What we do have is the skillset to take a non-educational profession or topic and spin it into education, or take it apart to find what could be useful in the classroom. Take the Chekhov's gun example- that's a theater idea given new life within a classroom. Your Teacher Brain should constantly be searching for ways to implement disparate ideas.

I tell this story in *He's the Weird Teacher*, but it's relevant so here it is again: I have a giant tattoo of a shark on my ribs. During the session I got to talking to the artist, and it turned out that he often went into his daughter's classroom to teach art lessons. During a moment when it stopped hurting enough that I could speak I asked him to come into my room, and he said he'd love to. We set it up and within a few weeks my class was being taught by a guy with a throat tattoo. He was great. The kids loved it. He talked about creativity and did an art lesson that I still do to this day. It's called Squiggle. Take a big piece of paper, make a quick squiggle across it, and then turn it this way and that until you see a picture in the squiggle, and draw it. So a quick wiggle of ink becomes an otter, a motorcycle, or a rock star. Don't let students get away with a worm or a snake or a wave. Those are too easy.

I never would have had this art lesson, a lesson I use for all kinds of things, if I hadn't looked outside traditional education avenues.

Joy

Teaching is a joyful profession. Students are hilarious. Allow yourself to feel the joy, and allow your students to feel it as well. Joy will solve a lot of problems in a classroom, and kids need to feel those emotions. Dance. Sing. Play. Allow yourself to be completely caught off guard and laugh until tears come. Not at a student, but with them. Joy will get you through the hard times. It's ok to be silly. Joy will help fight The Whatever. The Whatever is that shrug of apathy some teachers get as the year goes on. Find your joy, it will keep The Whatever at bay. Do not become one of those teachers who gets so beaten down they give up in the middle of a shrug.

The Long Game

Education is a long game. We often do not see the results of our labors. It's best to accept that now. But what you're doing in the moment still matters. Those lessons should be the best they can be because students need that information. You're teaching students how to learn, but you're also teaching concrete information. It's vital that students understand and respect the learning process, the scientific process, and know how to acquire knowledge on their own. There's a lot to our job. Students need to feel supported during the learning. They need to be learning how to learn. They need to be learning how to efficiently retain and recall information, as well as how to find new information, but they also need to know a lot of the things you will be teaching them. Have respect for not only the process, but also the in-the-moment act of learning and teaching.

Realize that much of what we do is seed-planting. Someone else will water those seeds. The student you had in your classroom is just starting out, and it's impossible to know where their journey will take them. Thinking in the long term will keep you sane when you're overwhelmed with the Now, and it will excite you when you see a student start to grab onto something.

Have a Hobby

Don't be consumed by teaching. There will always be more to do. There will always be more to grade, more to plan. Leave it be. It's not going anywhere. I worked with a teacher who set an alarm after school and when it went off, no matter what she was doing, she left. She went to the gym. Her health mattered to her.

The best teaching advice I ever got came during that nightmare time in that overflow combo class. A teacher I'd go to for help told me, "Have a hobby. Have a reason to leave, otherwise this job will eat you up." Don't be a martyr. Don't sacrifice your personal life to be a teacher. Teaching is part of you, it is not all of you. You'll never not be a teacher, but that should never be your total self-definition.

Sign Language

Mentor and Student Teachers- find a way to communicate that the kids will never pick up on. Come up with verbal shorthand, safe words, that have agreed upon meanings. Hand gestures that mean, "This lessons is starting to drag, get on with it," without having to point at your watch and make a "wrap it up" motion. Texting works great for this. If you've never texted a friend or significant other while in the same room with the person, congratulations on avoiding certain kinds of uncomfortable situations. We should be beyond having issues with people on their phones in school as long as they're on task, and that counts for teachers as well. Having some sort of silent communication in place will save headaches and confusion. Unless you forget what the signs mean, then your class turns into a comedy routine. Which is also fun.

Mr. Murphy

Mr. Murphy of Murphy's Law fame will always be with you. Prepare for him to mess with your technology, your lessons plans, your projects, your life in general. You will learn to tap dance around problems, and smile while doing it. You will learn to plan for every contingency, and then Mr. Murphy will throw something at you that you never thought possible. It's ok, that's why we get paid the big bucks. We're good at improvising around these things. You will also have to teach students this skill, because it's going to happen to them too. Be open and honest about it.

Sleep

Never underestimate the healing power of a good night's sleep. Or an after-school nap.

21. Educational Midwives

I have two children, and for both pregnancies we saw a midwife. While I'll never tell someone how to have their baby, I will say that going through that entire process with someone who was not a doctor or an OB, someone whose job it was to think about my wife's emotional condition along with her physical one (I know doctors and OBs do that too, but to a different degree), made the process an easier, more joyful, and a more comfortable one. During both births, but especially the second, I've never seen a more calm, collected human being. Which meant that in the middle of the birth of my second son I looked up at the midwife, up to her hips in the birthing tub, smiling and breathing and making calming word noises neither my wife nor I were processing in any reasonable way, and thought, "This woman would make an incredible kindergarten teacher." It came out of nowhere, as thoughts like that are often unbidden and flit through your brain just fast enough for you to register but not contemplate. And then he was in the world and I stopped thinking about teaching for a little while.

Our sons were born in two different states, in two different environments. Our oldest was born in a military hospital in Hawaii, the big pink one on the hill. Our second was born in a birthing center in a hippy-dippy little town in southern Oregon. In both places we had wonderful midwives. In both places they were with us the whole pregnancy, explaining things, making jokes, letting us pretend we knew what was going on, and holding our hands. They brought our boys into the world in ways that we specifically requested. We were never told what to do by our midwives, we worked together.

Mentor teachers are educational midwives. We are there through that final phase, and we bring a baby teacher into the world. The university is there, doing their job, checking their boxes, being the hospital. Even though the midwife has things under control, there are certain things the hospital needs to do. We can bring the teacher into the world, but the university needs to fill out the official form. We can say you're here, you're a teacher now, but it's the university that registers you with the government.

A mentor teacher should put a human face on education in a way a student teacher has never had before. When a student teacher looks at their mentor teacher, they might not be looking directly into the future, but into a possible future. A student teacher should look to us and want to follow in our footsteps in some form or fashion. Their classroom shouldn't be ours. I do not want my student teachers to teach like I do. I want my student teachers to think about teaching like I do. I want them to take the love and dedication and bits of insanity they see and find out how that looks in their world. I want to teach them the notes, but let them write their own music.

When I am done having a student teacher in my class, I am not done being a mentor teacher. That never stops. I will forever and always feel a responsibility to my student teachers.

When I was a lifeguard the veteran lifeguards would be given rookie guards. This was done without the rookie's knowledge. It would be the vet's job to take that rook under their flipper (lifeguards don't have wings, you see), be sure they felt a part of the whole, and that they were up on their skills. They weren't to tell the rookie this was their job. I was given a rookie who wasn't the best swimmer. I know it seems counterintuitive that a lifeguard wouldn't be a great swimmer, but he wasn't. He was passable, and could save others, but wasn't fast or pretty. I was, and we spent all summer working at his stroke until he was keeping up and looking good doing it. My job didn't end there. We'd keep in touch during the off-season as well, because to us lifeguarding should be more than a summer job. I want to be clear that this was in the BeforeTimes, and I couldn't just shoot him a text or a Facebook message. Those things hadn't been invented yet. I actually had to put pen to paper, or dial numbers on a telephone and then use it to speak to him with my voice. Crazy stuff. I know lifeguarding was where I learned to be a mentor. I had many great mentors, and I continue to rip them off (*read: be inspired by them*) to this day.

Which brings me to my two final acts as an official mentor teacher. They are always the same, and they're incredibly important to me.

The last thing I do with my class is read *Oh, The Places You'll Go* by Dr. Seuss, because it's the perfect book for endings. But not for my student teacher. I buy my student teacher a different iconic children's novel written by the incomparable Roald Dahl. Can you guess which book? It's not *Matilda.*

I buy *Charlie and the Chocolate Factory.* In it I highlight a few special lines. Lines made more perfect by Gene Wilder's delivery in the film, but he had perfect words to begin with.

"A grown-up won't listen to me; he won't learn. He will try to do things his own way, and not mine. So I have to have a child. I want a good sensible loving child, one to whom I can tell all my most precious sweet-making secrets."

The classroom is my Chocolate Factory, and it exists to bring joy and understanding to children. While Mr. Wonka doesn't want an adult who will deviate from his recipes, I don't want a person who will deviate from my philosophies. I want someone who will use what they learned to open their own candy factory.

The final act I undertake as an official mentor teacher is have this discussion with my student teacher: If they loved what we did, and if they truly believed it helped them and made them better, if they want to honor how I tried to teach them and what they learned with me, they must do one thing. When they feel confident in their own abilities, in five or seven or ten years, they must seek to take on their own student teacher. The student must become the mentor. They must pay it forward and throw another pebble into the water. They must make new ripples.

Thank you for student teaching and joining this family. Thank you for mentor teaching and growing and strengthening our family.

Thank you.

Acknowledgements

In the spirit of this book, I'll start out by thanking the student teachers I've had so far- Bethany, Matt, Veronica, and Jill. Without you four my teaching wouldn't be what it is, and this book would not be possible. Thank you for what you taught me about being a teacher and for what you gave the students we shared. It was a pleasure and an honor to be there at the start of your journey. You know what I expect of you going forward.

Thank also to the University of the Pacific, who gave me an education, and the Universities of Hawaii and Portland, who gave me a chance to pay it forward with your student teachers. A preemptive thank you to them and every other university who has accepted this book into your teacher prep courses. *long significant look*

Thank you to Jennifer Paulson Thomas, who let me into her classroom when I was a baby teacher, and met me for dinner when I was overwhelmed with my own students. We haven't stayed in touch over the years, but I hope that you've taken in more student teachers.

This book would not be possible without my wife, who is more patient with me than anyone would think possible. I promise, now that this book is done, it'll be a year or two before I disappear upstairs into my office as soon as the kids go to bed every single night to pound away at another book. You never get the time you deserve, and at the same time you make every student teacher I drag home feel welcome. Also to my two Weirdlings who are insane and wonderful and who keep Daddy from drifting away into his own head all the time. Love you all.

A million thanks to the beta readers that made this book better than I ever could have alone- Sarah Windisch, Veronica Miller, Jessie Koch, Karen Lafferty, and David Saunders. Every writer needs extra eyes and smarter brains and I couldn't have asked for better.

Thank you to Ray Charbonneau and Y42K Publishing for being so easy to work with and for helping me to get the Weird into the world for yet another book. And Dorothy Dean Photography for yet another incredible cover.

This book was written over the summer of 2017, so thanks to everyone I hung out with during that time for pretending not to notice I was constantly writing and rewriting in my head (or on my phone).

Thanks to Pelican, Giraffes? Giraffes!, Russian Circles, and Joe Satriani for giving me an instrumental soundtrack to write to, and Henry Rollins, Nick Cave, Neko Case, Devin Townsend, and Chuck D for the voices that inspire, motivate, and get me through the hard parts. And to Travis Beacham and Guillermo del Toro for PACIFIC RIM. It inspires me every day.

Finally, thank you to every student who has shared my classroom. It's your world.

About the Author

Doug Robertson is a career classroom teacher currently residing just outside of Portland, OR with his understanding wife, two energetic children, and vaguely apathetic dog.

He has taught in California, Hawaii, and Oregon in grades 3, 4, 5, and 6. His whole career his principals have thought it would be funny to tease him about teaching kindergarten. He is not amused.

Thus far in his career he's had four student teachers, and is about to welcome two more into his room.

In addition to teaching, Doug speaks at teaching conferences and runs school- and district-wide professional developments. He is known generally as The Weird Teacher, a nickname given to him by two kindergarteners.

When not teaching, writing, parenting, or husbanding Doug sleeps, listens to the rock and roll music on his record player, or rides his motorcycle. He is the author of two other education books, *He's the Weird Teacher* and *THE Teaching Text (You're Welcome)*, and one novel, *The Unforgiving Road.* If you haven't read those you should, they're great.

He is both handsome and modest. He loves all teachers but has a special place in his heart for education students, and is happy to answer any questions that may have come from this book, or on issues that were left out. To ask questions, make comments, or inquire about having him come speak at your school, district, conference, or backyard BBQ can reach him at theweirdteacher@gmail.com and also on the twitter machine at @TheWeirdTeacher.

Teach with joy, love, and insanity.

The Drift

BONUS ESSAY!

"A bonus essay?" you ask. "How could this be possible?" It's quite simple. You see, this book effectively ends at the close of Educational Midwives. If you never read past that chapter, you've read the whole book. But for those of you brave enough to read beyond the end I have included this admittedly self-indulgent essay. In writing it I get a chance to talk about two of my favorite subjects- the student teacher/mentor teacher relationship and the 2013 film ***PACIFIC RIM****. It's not included in the main text of the book because it doesn't need to be, it's a stand-alone essay that I've added because sometimes a little self-indulgence is fun. It's also incredibly nerdy because I love thinking deeply about the media I love and mining it for all the meaning therein.*

Guillermo del Toro's 2013 robots, excuse me, mecha vs monsters blockbuster **PACIFIC RIM** is a lot of things. It's a well-made kaiju film. It's a fun action movie. It's a deceptively smart, heart-filled science fiction movie wrapped in a candy coating of mecha-punching-monsters.

On the surface, it does not seem like a perfect parallel for the student teacher/mentor teacher relationship. But that's exactly what it is.

For the poor unfortunates among you who have not yet borne witness to **PACIFIC RIM**, here's a quick breakdown- monsters known as kaiju have begun emerging from a breach deep in the Pacific Ocean. To battle against the kaiju and preserve the human race, the nations of the world band together to build Jaegers, which are giant mecha. Mecha are different from robots in that robots run on their own, mecha require a human to pilot them. In the case of **PACIFIC RIM**'s Jaegers, two pilots are required because of their massive size. And this is where things get interesting. In order to effectively pilot a Jaeger, the two pilots mind-meld through what's called The Drift. In the Drift each pilot knows exactly what the other is thinking and feeling. There are no secrets in the Drift. Our two leads, a veteran Jaeger pilot named Raleigh and a rookie pilot named Mako, are Drift compatible and become co-pilots of a Jaeger named Gipsy Danger. Through the combination of Raleigh's experience and Mako's training and familiarity with their rebuilt Jaeger, they are able to achieve together what neither could alone and *spoiler alert* save the day.

Raleigh and Mako's relationship is the perfect mentor teacher/student teacher relationship. Raleigh knows how things go in the real world and has experience thinking on his feet and improvising around unexpected developments. But, for reasons best left unspoiled, he's been out of touch and isn't up on all the latest Jaeger developments. Mako knows the Jaeger training manual backward and forward. She's up on all the tech, but she's never put it into practice in the real world. In order to be successful, each has to let their egos go and fully trust one another.

Like many of our incoming student teachers, Mako Mori is an excellent student with a difficult background. Not all teachers were good students, and not all teachers go into the profession because they liked school. Some go in because they didn't like school and they know they could make it better. As a child, Mako was traumatized by a kaiju. Rather than run from it her whole life, she took the only course that would allow her to confront her problem on equal footing and see that others wouldn't suffer as she did. Her training tells her she is ready. She's great in the simulator. However, as soon as Mako gets her chance, her past comes back to bite her and she freezes. It's a catastrophe. All her training couldn't prepare her for what it was really like in a Jaeger. Student teachers come from university full of Methods and Theories, ready to get in front of students. They are often quickly confronted with the hard reality that book learning and classroom learning are two completely different things. Sometimes a struggle they had when they were students comes back to them as teachers. "Oh great, I have to teach grammar. I hated grammar." They stumble and fail.

Raleigh is a mentor teacher for Mako. He's the one who has been there, though being there has left some scars. It's how you deal with those scars that matters. Raleigh deals with them by making his first order of business letting Mako cover his weaker side, admitting that he needs her and, before they've even Drifted, trusting her. Mentor teachers must give student teachers the benefit of the doubt, trust their training even when we know it's not enough on its own. And when Mako goes off the rails, Raleigh is there sharing every moment, watching, learning, talking her through it. When it's over he doesn't chastise her. They sit together and have an open and honest conversation about what went wrong and why. Rather than make her feel terrible about her failure, Raleigh uses it to make Mako a better pilot and to bring them closer. Student teachers will fail, sometimes catastrophically. What's important is to recognize that this happens, and use it to move forward.

Mako and Raleigh do normal human things together. They go to lunch. They chat. They learn who they are beyond being

Jaeger pilots, because that knowledge will ultimately serve them as Jaeger pilots. Mentor teachers and student teachers should have some kind of a relationship that extends beyond the walls of the school. Getting to know each other as people will aid them in working and planning together. It will help mentor teachers see how best to communicate with the student teacher, and vice versa.

Mako and Raleigh even work together against the administration, who isn't so sure this is the correct pairing. Raleigh goes to the mat for Mako. Mentor teachers should be defenders of our student teachers. They're our responsibility. To protect. To vouch for. To support in all ways.

Through these bonding moments, Raleigh and Mako learn to work together and shore up each other's weaknesses. A student teacher should not be subordinate to a mentor teacher. They are partners. When they are working together, in the Drift, is when the classroom runs best. Through time, talk, and troubles a mentor teacher and student teacher will learn what the other needs and how best to give them that. The classroom becomes a dance, unspoken communication flowing easily.

On top of this, it's Mako who teaches Raleigh things he didn't know. When confronted with a problem he has no answers to, Mako steps in to show the older man that kids today know some things too. Our student teachers come to use with background in things we don't know because research has been moving forward while we've been teaching. We try to keep up, of course, but students get the freshest information. Listening when they suggest one more thing could mean the difference between a lesson crashing to the ground or being saved at the last minute.

The ultimate goal of the mentor teacher/student teacher

relationship is the Drift. It's finding a place of equality in which the classroom seems like it couldn't possibly be run with only one of you. It's finding a closeness you didn't expect by sharing freely and opening your heart and mind to the other person. An effective Jaeger is one that is powered not by nuclear turbines or one personality overwhelming the other, but by friendship and respect. An effective classroom is not built on fear or blame or unbalanced power, but one where partner teachers find a relationship built on those same principles of friendship and respect.

My student teachers can always find me in the Drift.

78810700R00127

Made in the USA
Lexington, KY
14 January 2018